Mastering IPv6

From Addressing Basics to

Advanced

Deployment Techniques

Copyright Page

publisher are not responsible for errors, inaccuracies, or omissions. They shall not be liable for any loss or damage of any kind, including but not limited to, any direct, indirect, incidental, consequential, special, or exemplary damages arising from or in connection with the use of this book or its information.

Published by Kevogo Musudia

Who Is This Book For?

Mastering IPv6: From Addressing Basics to Advanced Deployment Techniques is designed to serve a broad range of users who are interested in different facets of IT and networking. Network managers, engineers, and architects will gain a thorough understanding of IPv6 addressing concepts, enabling them to create and oversee orderly, effective IP network architectures. A useful tool for comprehending how appropriate addressing enhances resource usage, security, and overall network performance will be acquired by IT administrators and decision-makers.

This book offers a solid basis for understanding and teaching addressing ideas, making it appropriate for both IT students and educators. Experts in cloud computing and virtualization, system administrators, and network security will find useful information relevant to their fields. The book's clear explanations and useful examples will also be helpful to IPv6 transition planners and network enthusiasts who want to learn more about IPv6 addressing.

What can you expect?

Mastering IPv6: From Addressing Basics to Advanced Deployment Techniques guarantees accessibility and clarity when navigating the complex world of IP addressing. Readers of all experience levels may anticipate clear explanations and useful examples that support comprehension and implementation. IPv6 addressing is thoroughly covered in the book, along with Subnetting, Routing, Security, and Transition Mechanisms. It offers an all-encompassing method for utilizing subnetting for scalable, secure, and well-organized network architectures, with an emphasis on best practices for network design, troubleshooting insights, and real-world case studies. Readers will remain ahead of the curve in the ever-evolving world of networking thanks to the discussion of future trends and considerations and the relevance of subnetting in developing technologies. This guide is a great resource for anyone looking to become an expert in IPv6 addressing.

Why IP Addressing?

The fundamental structure for identifying and locating devices on a network is provided by IP addressing. The shortcomings of IPv4 are addressed by IPv6, the next generation of the Internet Protocol, particularly the exhaustion of addresses. The requirement for a larger address space to handle the increasing number of connected devices, especially with the introduction of the Internet of Things (IoT), is what is driving the switch to IPv6.

There is practically an endless supply of unique addresses available with IPv6 due to its large address space. This abundance is important because there are an increasing number of internet-connected devices—from computers and smartphones to smart appliances, sensors, and other IoT devices—on the market. With IPv6 in place, every device will be able to have a globally unique address, improving end-to-end connection and enabling effective Internet communication.

Furthermore, network administration and security are enhanced with IPv6. It has features like integrated IPsec, which improves the security of online communication. IPv6's streamlined header layout simplifies routing procedures, improving packet processing and lowering network device overhead.

Network administrators, engineers, and architects must comprehend IP addressing, especially IPv6, to construct and oversee contemporary networks. To maintain the internet's development and viability, IPv6 must eventually be implemented, and successfully navigating these changes requires a thorough understanding of IP addressing. This entails understanding not just the fundamentals of IP addressing but also more complex ideas like subnetting, which is essential for optimizing network architecture and address distribution. A firm understanding of IP addressing, with a particular emphasis on IPv6, is essential for developing resilient, expandable, and future-ready network infrastructures in the ever-changing field of networking.

Table of Content

Chapter 1: IPv6 Addressing

1.1 Introduction

IPv6 (Internet Protocol version 6) has emerged as a crucial option to solve the shortcomings of IPv4 in the quickly changing networking landscape. The adoption of IPv6 has become essential for the continued growth of the digital ecosystem due to the proliferation of internet-connected devices and the expiration of IPv4 addresses. The vast address space that IPv6 offers an enormously higher number of unique addresses than IPv4 which is essential for supporting the constantly growing number of devices, services, and users on the worldwide network.

This shift is a strategic requirement for guaranteeing the scalability, security, and effective operation of contemporary networks, not just a technical one. This introduction lays the groundwork for understanding IPv6's importance in addressing the needs of modern networking, where reliable security, smooth connectivity, and effective resource allocation are critical.

1.2 IPv6 Address format

IPv6 addresses differ from their IPv4 counterparts in that they have a unique structure. Compared to IPv4 addresses, which are 32 bits long, IPv6 addresses are 128 bits long. A substantially bigger address space is made possible by this lengthened protocol, offering an almost limitless number of distinct addresses. IPv6 addresses use hexadecimal notation, which allows each number to represent four bits, to express these 128 bits.

Eight groups, each having four hexadecimal numbers, make up the hexadecimal representation. A structure that improves readability and makes manual entry easier is created by separating these groupings with colons. The format for writing IPv6 address is:x:x:x:x:x:x:x:x, where each "x" is made up of four hexadecimal places. An IPv4 address's eight bits are referred to as an octet. A segment of 16 bits, or four hexadecimal values, is referred to as a hextet in IPv6. Four hexadecimal digits, or 16 bits, make up each "x," which represents a single hextet.

Hexadecimal digits are represented by the letters A-F and the numerals 0-9 and range from 0 to 15.

For example, 'a' stands for 10, 'b' for 11, 'c' for 12, and so on.

An example of an IPv6 address would be as follows:

2001:0DB8: ACAD: 0001:0000:0000: 0000:00001

Observation:

There are:

i. 8 groups of 4 hexadecimal digits.
ii. Each group is made up of 16 bits (4 hexadecimal places * 4 bits).
iii. ":" is the separator.
iv. Hex digits are not case-insensitive, "ACAD" can be written as "acad" or "ACad"...

The IPv6 address is composed of 128 bits, of which each group represents 16 bits.

A 128-bit IPv6 address is composed of two parts. The prefix refers to the first 64 bits. The network and subnet addresses are included in the prefix. Since addresses are assigned according to their actual locations, global routing information is also included in the prefix. It's common to refer to the 64-bit prefix as the global routing prefix.

The interface ID is the final 64 bits which makes the interface's specific address.

1.2.1 Do not include leading zeros

An IPv6 address can have consecutive groups of zeros compressed to improve readability and eliminate redundancy.

2001:0DB8: ACAD: 0001:0000:0000: 0000:00001 can be represented as 2001:DB8: ACAD: 1:0:0:0:1

06df can be represented as 6df

0e00 can be represented as e00

To avoid ambiguity in the address, this restriction ONLY applies to leading zeros and NOT to trailing zeros. For instance, the values "0bcd" and "bcd0," although could represent the same value, are not equivalent to the hexadecimal "bcd."

1.2.2 Double colon usage

The second guideline to help simplify ipv6 addresses is that any single, continuous string of one or more 16-bit hexadecimal hexets that are all zeros can be substituted with a double colon (::). 2001:DB8: ACAD: 1:0:0:0:1, for instance, might be written as 2001:DB8: ACAD:1::1 (leading 0s omitted). The three all-0 hextets (0:0:0) are substituted with a double colon (::)

A case in point of the double colon being used incorrectly is as follows: 2001:DB8::ACAD:1::1

In an address, the double colon (::) can only be used once; otherwise, many addresses could be generated. The notation of ipv6 addresses can frequently be significantly decreased when combined with the eliminating leading 0s approach. This format is often referred to as compressed.

In summary, the ipv6 address structure uses a 128-bit hexadecimal format that is divided into eight groups and separated by colons. In addition to supporting a far bigger address space, this approach improves the efficiency and clarity of addressing in the context of contemporary networking.

1.3 IPv6 Address Types

Different types of IPv6 addresses exist, and each has a distinct function in network communication. The following are the primary categories of IPv6 addresses:

i. **Unicast**: A device's single network interface is identified by a unicast address.

   a. When a device sends data to a unicast address on the network, it is specifically targeting another device.

   b. Within IPv6, a unicast address can be either local, restricted to a single network, or global, making it unique throughout the entire Internet.

ii. **Multicast**: When several devices want to receive the same data, they can be identified by their IPv6 multicast address. Multicast addresses are intended to represent a collection of devices, as opposed to unicast addresses, which identify a single device. The multicast group can be joined by devices that want to receive data transmitted to a multicast address.

iii. **Anycast**: Anycast is a network addressing and routing technique that sends data to the closest recipient among a set of possible recipients from a single sender. Anycast addresses are used in the context of IPv6 to designate a group of devices, and data is transmitted to the closest device in that group. Anycast differs from unicast and multicast in that it allows for the assignment of a single anycast address to several devices, with the routing infrastructure selecting the precise device that will receive the data.

1.3.1 Types of IPv6 Unicast Addresses

i. **Global Unicast Address**

Global unicast IPv6 addresses are globally routable on the Internet, just as public IPv4 addresses. These addresses are exclusive to the IPv6 network worldwide and are given by Internet authority. Devices connected to several networks communicate with one another using global unicast addresses.

A typical illustration of an IPv6 address that is used in documentation is as follows:

2001:0DB8: ACAD: 0010:0000:000: 0000:0001

To better comprehend it, let's dissect it.

- **2001: ODB8: ACAD:** The first 48 bits represent the Global Routing prefix.
- **0010**: The next 16 bits represent the Subnet ID.
- **0000:000:0000:0001**: The last 64-bit represents the Interface ID.

In the production network, these addresses might be given to internet-connected gadgets so they can connect anywhere in the world. Notably, IPv6 addresses have a substantially bigger address space than IPv4 addresses due to their enormous length, which is beneficial for the increasing number of devices on the internet.

ii. **Link-Local Unicast Address**

It is not routable outside of the local network and is automatically configured by the device. On the same local network (link), this kind of address is utilized for communication, and link-local addresses are frequently utilized for neighbor discovery and first contact.

A few simple illustrations of Link-Local Addresses in IPv6 are as follows:

Link-local address using the value 1 for the interface identifier.

fe80::1

The use of MAC address-based identifiers demonstrated by a link-local address with a longer interface identification is as follows:

fe80::0002:c7ff:fe80: a7e4

If you wish to indicate the link-local IPv6 address linked to a particular network interface.

fe80::%eth0

%eth0: The network interface to which the link-local address is assigned is specified by the %eth0 portion. The word "interface" in networking refers to a device's network connection, which is frequently represented by a virtual interface or a physical port (such as an Ethernet port).

The "fe80" prefix serves as a link-local address's key identifier. These addresses are mostly used for local network segment communication, and they are automatically configured on network interfaces if there isn't a globally routable address available.

iii. **Unique Local Unicast Address (ULA)**

IPv6 addresses designated for private usage within a company or location are known as Unique Local Addresses or ULAs. You may compare them with IPv4 private addresses such as 192.168.0.10. They are not routable on the Internet; instead, they are utilized within a particular site or organization. Within an organization, private addressing schemes can be created with the help of ULAs.

The range of Unique local addresses are from (fc00: :/7 to fdff: :/7)

For local addressing within a site or between a small number of locations, unique local addresses are utilized.

For devices that will never need to connect to another network, unique local addresses can be used.

There is no global routing or translation of unique local addresses to a global IPv6 address.

To safeguard or conceal their network from possible security threats, numerous websites also make use of the private character of RFC 1918 addresses. However, the IETF has long advised that sites implement the necessary security measures on their internet-facing router, as this was never the intended usage of these technologies.

A Unique Local Addresses (ULAs) format of the IPv6 address is as follows:

fc00: cafe:6595::1

This syntax can be used, similarly to the link-local example, to specify the ULA linked to a specific network interface, such as "eth0."

fd00: %eth0

The reserved ULA prefix includes the "fd" at the start of the address. The network and interface identifiers are assigned to the bits that follow.

For example, you may designate a Unique Local Address range if you wish to use IPv6 when setting up a private network within your company. After that, devices connected to your network would receive addresses from this range, enabling internal communication without requiring them to be directly reachable from the public internet.

iv. **Loopback Address**

The loopback address in IPv6 is represented by::1. This address is the same as 127.0.0.1, the IPv4 loopback address. For testing and troubleshooting purposes, it enables a device to send network traffic to itself.

It is used to test network-related features on a single device, independent of other networks.

The illustration below is a command utility for testing internal paths through the TCP/IP protocols that are working.

Microsoft Windows [Version 10.0.19045.3803]

(c) Microsoft Corporation. All rights reserved.

C:\Users\KM-PC>**ping ::1**

Pinging::1 with 32 bytes of data:

Reply from ::1: time<1ms

Reply from ::1: time<1ms

Reply from ::1: time<1ms

Reply from ::1: time<1ms

Ping statistics for:1:

Packets: Sent = 4, Received = 4, Lost = 0 (0% loss),

Approximate round trip times in milli-seconds:

Minimum = 0ms, Maximum = 0ms, Average = 0ms

C:\Users\KM-PC>

When testing if network services are operating properly on a local workstation without requiring external connections, developers and network administrators can use the loopback address as a convenient tool.

1.3.2 Multicast address

Multicast addresses for IPv6 are similar to those of IPv4.Sending a single packet to one or more destinations (multicast group) requires the use of a multicast address. Multicast IPv6 addresses begin with the prefix ff00: :/8 Multicast addresses cannot be source addresses, they can only be destination addresses.

IPv6 multicast addresses are divided into two types as follows:

i. **Well-known Multicast addresses**

Multicast addresses that are reserved for certain groups of devices are known as assigned multicast addresses. A single address used to connect to a collection of devices sharing a protocol or service is known as an allocated multicast address. Multicast addresses that are assigned are used in conjunction with particular protocols, like DHCPv6.

The most widely used IPv6-assigned multicast groups are as follows:

- **ff02::1 All-nodes multicast group**: This is a multicast group that all IPv6-enabled devices join; a packet sent to this group is received and processed by all IPv6 interfaces on the link or network, resulting in an effect similar to an IPv4 broadcast address. The figure illustrates how an IPv6 router can communicate with an all-node multicast address by sending ICMPv6 RA messages to the all-node multicast group.

- **ff02::2 All-routers multicast group**: IPv6 routers are members of this multicast group, which they use to communicate. When a router is given the ipv6 unicast-routing global configuration command to enable IPv6, it joins this group immediately. Upon transmission to this group, every IPv6 router within the network or connection receives and processes the packet.

IPv6 All-Nodes Multicast: RA Message

The all-routers multicast address receives icmpv6 RS messages from IPv6-enabled devices. To help the device with configuration, the RS message asks the IPv6 router for help and sends an RA message. An RA message is returned from the IPv6 router.

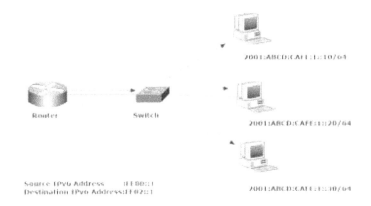

ii. **Solicited node multicast addresses**

The all-nodes multicast address and the solicited-node multicast address are comparable. A solicited-node multicast address has the benefit of being mapped to a unique Ethernet multicast address. This enables the Ethernet NIC to filter the frame and determine whether the device is the intended recipient of the IPv6 packet by looking at the destination MAC address without forwarding it to the IPv6 process.

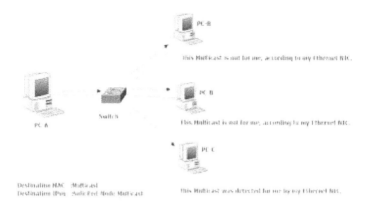

- **ff02::9**

  The multicast address for RIPng (Routing Information Protocol next generation). used for communications about routing.

- **ff02::16**

  Multicast Listener Discovery version 2 (MLDv2) multicast address for controlling membership in multicast groups.

Uses of IPv6 Multicast Addresses

i. **Routing Protocols**: Routing protocols frequently use multicast, which makes it possible for routers to effectively communicate routing information.

ii. **Multimedia Streaming**: To broadcast multimedia content to numerous recipients at once, IPv6 multicast is used.

iii. **Network Management**: Multicast can be used for operations related to network management, like sending software updates or configuration data to numerous devices.

iv. **IPv6 Neighbor Discovery**: Neighbor Solicitation and Advertisement tasks in IPv6 use multicast addresses, which enable devices to find and connect with neighbors on the same channel.

IPv6 multicast addresses begin with the prefix ff02::/16 at all times. The multicast group's type and scope are determined by the last 32 bits of the particular group identifier.

Designing and executing effective and scalable communication in IPv6 networks requires an understanding of IPv6 multicast addresses, especially in situations where data delivery to several recipients at once is required.

1.3.3 Anycast address

Anycast addresses in IPv6 are expressed using the same standard IPv6 notation as unicast addresses. The difference is not in their format, but rather in how they are assigned and used.

This is a quick summary of IPv6 address representation and how anycast works with it:

i. **IPv6 Address Format**

An IPv6 address is represented by eight groups of four hexadecimal numbers separated by colons, and it has a length of 128 bits. For example: 2001: ODB8: ACAD: 0000:0000:0000: 0000:0004.

ii. **Anycast Prefix**

The unicast address space is used to allocate an IPv6 anycast address. There isn't a particular "anycast address range." Rather, the entire IPv6 address space is used to obtain an anycast address.

iii. Assignment

Several nodes and/or interfaces are given Anycast addresses. Usually, these nodes are dispersed throughout the network infrastructure.

iv. Routing

Packets submitted to an anycast address are routed to the closest node that possesses that address thanks to anycast routing protocols. The routing distance or other pertinent metrics are used to determine this.

Illustration:

Let us examine an instance where a website employs anycast as its DNS server.

There could be several DNS servers with the same anycast IPv6 address spread around the globe.

A DNS query sent by a user's device to the anycast address is forwarded, according to routing protocol and network constraints, to the closest DNS server.

Example of Representation:

Anycast DNS Server 1: 2001:0DB8::1

Anycast DNS Server 2: 2001:0DB8::1

Anycast DNS Server 3: 2001:0DB8::1

The anycast address of each of the three DNS servers in this case is the same. By routing a DNS query to the closest DNS server when a user's device sends one to 2001:0db8::1, speed is improved and latency is decreased.

Uses of IPv6 Anycast Addresses:

   i. DNS Services

   To increase the availability and responsiveness of DNS queries, DNS servers frequently employ Anycast.

   ii. Content Delivery Networks (CDNs)

   To distribute content more quickly and closer to users, CDNs may employ anycast.

   iii. Network Services

   To divide traffic among several instances, Anycast can be used for a variety of network services, including load balancers.

Designing robust and effective network topologies with IPv6 requires an understanding of anycast, particularly in situations where proximity-based routing, load distribution, and redundancy are essential.

Chapter 2: IPv6 Subnetting

One essential component of administering and making the most of the enormous address space that Internet Protocol version 6 offers is IPv6 subnetting. As IPv4 addresses run out, IPv6 has become the replacement, providing an exponentially bigger pool of unique addresses. To effectively distribute addresses inside a network, IPv6 subnetting divides the massive 128-bit address space into smaller, more manageable pieces. In contrast to IPv4, which makes extensive use of subnet masks, IPv6 uses a hexadecimal representation for addresses and offers a simplified notation known as CIDR (Classless Inter-Domain Routing). Network administrators and engineers must comprehend IPv6 subnetting to build scalable and well-organized networks that can meet the ever-increasing needs of the contemporary Internet environment.

2.1 Subnet Using the Subnet ID

Remember that in IPv4, subnets are created by borrowing bits from the host portion. This is because IPv4 subnetting was an afterthought. Subnetting was considered during the design of IPv6.Subnets are created in the IPv6 Global Unicast Address (GUA) using a distinct subnet ID field. The space between the interface ID and the global routing prefix is the subnet ID field, as shown in the figure.

For any network, a 128-bit address provides the benefit of supporting a sizable number of subnets and hosts within each subnet. Address conservation is not an issue. For example, a 16-bit subnet ID will be produced if the global routing prefix is /48 and the interface ID is 64 bits:

A 16-bit subnet ID can be used to generate 65,536 subnets.

With a 64-bit interface ID, a subnet can handle up to 18 quintillion host IPv6 addresses (18,000,000,000,000,000,000).

Although it is not always necessary, subnetting into the 64-bit interface ID, commonly known as the host part, is also an option.

Because IPv6 subnetting does not involve binary conversion, it is also simpler to construct than IPv4 subnetting. Just add up the hexadecimal numbers to find the next available subnet.

Illustration I

IPv6 subnetting

Assume, for instance, that a company has been given the global routing prefix 2001:0db8:cafe::/48 together with a 16-bit subnet ID. As seen in the diagram below, this would enable the company to build $2^{16} = 65,536$ subnets. Observe that every subnet has the same global routing prefix. For every subnet, the subnet ID hextet is increased in hexadecimal.

Using a 16-bit Subnet ID for subnetting

2001:0db8: cafe:**0000**: :/64

2001:0db8: cafe:**0001**: :/64

2001:0db8: cafe:**0002**: :/64

2001:0db8: cafe:**0003**: :/64

2001:0db8: cafe:**0004**: :/64

2001:0db8: cafe:**0005**: :/64

2001:0db8: cafe:**0006**: :/64

2001:0db8: cafe:**0007**: :/64

2001:0db8: cafe:**0008**: :/64

2001:0db8: cafe:**0009**: :/64

2001:0db8: cafe:**000a**: :/64

2001:0db8: cafe:**000b**: :/64

2001:0db8: cafe:**000c**: :/64

2001:0db8: cafe:**000d**: :/64

2001:0db8: cafe:**000e**: :/64

2001:0db8: cafe:**000f**: :/64

subnets 16 up to the last subnet not shown…

2001:0db8: cafe: **ffff**::/64 (this is the last subnet)

Illustration II

Let's examine an IPv6 subnetting example to show how a given address space can be effectively divided into smaller subnets. Assume that within an enterprise, for various reasons, we would like to subnet the given IPv6 block 2001:0db8:cafe:1004::/64.

Let us establish three subnets:

Subnet 1 (Purchasing Department):

Subnet ID: 2001:0db8: cafe:1004: :/64

Subnet Range: 2001:0db8: cafe:1004::1 to 2001:0db8: cafe: 1004::ffff/64

This subnet is dedicated to the Purchasing department.

Subnet 2 (Operations Department):

Subnet ID: 2001:0db8:cafe:1005::/64

Subnet Range: 2001:0db8:cafe:1005::1 to 2001:0db8:cafe:1005::ffff/64

This subnet is designated for the Operations department.

Subnet 3 (Marketing Department):

Subnet ID: 2001:0db8:cafe:1006::/64

Subnet Range: 2001:0db8:cafe:1006::1 to 2001:0db8:cafe:1006::ffff/64

This subnet is designated for the Operations department.

There are numerous alternative host addresses inside each subnet in this example because each subnet has a unique /64 prefix. Each subnet may support a large number of devices since the remaining 64 bits of an IPv6 address are reserved for host addresses. This IPv6 address allocation helps organizations organize and maintain their network infrastructure more effectively.

IPv6 Subnet Allocation

With over 65,536 subnets to choose from, the network administrator's task becomes developing a logical scheme to address the network.

For the sample topology depicted in the image, five subnets are required: one for each LAN and one for the serial link between R1 and R2. Unlike the example for IPv4, with IPv6, the serial link subnet will have the same prefix length as the LANs. This may seem to "waste" addresses while using IPv6, however, it has no bearing on address conservation.

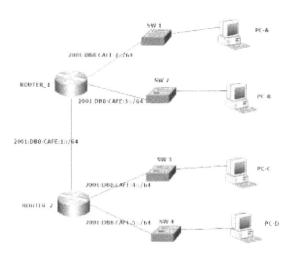

The diagram above shows, the five IPv6 subnets assigned; in this instance, subnet ID fields 0001 through 0005 were used. Each /64 subnet will have more addresses available than could ever be needed.

IPv6 address assignment strategies

This entails the allocation of IPv6 addresses to various organizations, end users, and Internet service providers (ISPs). Compared to IPv4, IPv6 has a substantially bigger address space, giving address assignment schemes greater design flexibility.

Several popular methods for assigning IPv6 addresses are as follows:

i. **Provider-based Unicast Addressing**

ISPs allocate IPv6 address blocks to their clients per the quantity of address space such clients need.

The IPv6 address space is utilized like the IPv4 provider-based addressing model

ii. **Geographical Assignment**

Devices within a particular region can share a similar address prefix by assigning IPv6 addresses based on geographical regions.

This approach can support network design and debugging as well as efficient address allocation management.

iii. **Hierarchical Addressing**

Hierarchical addressing structures can be created by organizations to make network management easier.

Subnets can be established according to departments, organizational units, or physical locations.

iv. **Dynamic Host Configuration Protocol version 6 (DHCPv6)**

IPv6 addresses can be dynamically assigned to hosts inside a network using DHCPv6.

In situations where static addressing might not be feasible, DHCPv6 can offer more flexibility when it comes to managing address assignments.

v. **Stateless Address Autoconfiguration (SLAAC)**

Without the use of a DHCPv6 server, hosts can automatically configure their IPv6 addresses through the use of SLAAC. IPv6 addresses are formed by hosts using data gathered through router advertisements.

vi. **Privacy Extensions**

By creating temporary addresses regularly, IPv6 privacy extensions give individual devices a measure of anonymity.

Incoming connections may still use a stable address, but outgoing connections may utilize short-lived addresses.

Note: Additional assignments include IPv6 subnetting, Link-Local Addressing, Global Unicast Addressing, and Multicast Addressing, all of which we have already covered.

Strategies for assigning IPv6 addresses can differ depending on the objectives and particular needs of the network or organization. Combining these approaches to handle various facets of network design and administration is a typical practice.

2.1 Static Global Unicast Address Configuration (GUA)

An IPv6 address must be manually assigned to an interface to configure a static Global Unicast Address (GUA) on a router. Routable addresses on the Internet that are utilized for communication throughout the worldwide IPv6 network are called global unicast addresses.

Scenario

In this scenario, we will set up a router, switch, and two PCs for manual IPv6 configuration. Let's assume for the sake of simplicity that the PCs are already physically connected to the switch and that the router and switch are already connected.

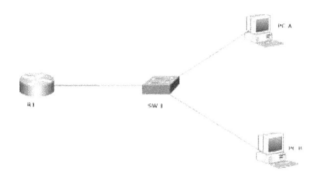

Router: R1

Interface: GigabitEthernet0/0

IPv6 Address: 2001:db8:acad:1::1/64

Switch: SW1

Interface: Vlan 1

IPv6 Address: 2001:db8:acad:1::2/64

Computer: PCA

Network Interface: Fast Ethernet

IPv6 Address: 2001:db8:acad:1::3/64

Default Gateway:2001:db8:acad:1::1

Computer:PCB

Network Interface: Fast Ethernet

IPv6 Address: 2001:db8:acad:1::4/64

Default Gateway:2001:db8: acad:1::1

Description	Command
Get into the interface configuration mode of R1.	R1(config)#interface g0/0
Configure the assigned IPv6 address on the Router's interface.	R1(config)#interface g0/0 R1(config-if)#ipv6 address fe80::1:1 link-local R1(config-if)#end
Configure the assigned IPv6 address on the Switch VLAN Interface. Note: Remember to enable IPv6 capabilities.	SW1(config)#sdm prefer dual-ipv4-and-ipv6 default SW1(config)#end SW1#reload SW1(config)#interface vlan 1 SW1(config-if)#ipv6 address fe80::1:2 link-local SW1(config-if) #end
Configure the assigned IPv6 address on PCA	IPv6 address: fe80::1:3
Configure assigned IPv6 address on PCB	IPv6 address: fe80::1:4
To verify the configuration of the Router and/or Switch	R1#show ipv6 interface brief SW1#show ipv6 interface brief

2.2 Static Link-Local Unicast Address Configuration

The command ipv6 address ipv6-link-local-address link-local can be used to manually configure LLAs. The link-local parameter has to come after the address if it starts with this hextet and falls between fe80 and febf.

Scenario

Let's use the same topology we have experimented with before of a router, switch, and two PCs. Let's assume for the sake of simplicity that the PCs are already physically connected to the switch and that the router and switch are already connected.

Router: R1

Interface: GigabitEthernet0/0

IPv6 Address: FE80::1:1

Switch: SW1

Interface: Vlan 1

IPv6 Address: FE80::1:2

Computer: PCA

Network Interface: Fast Ethernet

IPv6 Address: FE80::1:3

Computer: PCB

Network Interface: Fast Ethernet

IPv6 Address: FE80::1:4

Description	Command
Get into the interface configuration mode of R1.	R1(config)#interface g0/0
Configure the assigned IPv6 link-local address on the Router's interface.	R1(config)#interface g0/0 R1(config-if)#ipv6 address 2001:db8:acad:1::1/64
Configure the assigned IPv6llink local address on the Switch VLAN Interface. Note: Remember to enable IPv6 capabilities.	SW1(config)#sdm prefer dual-ipv4-and-ipv6 default SW1(config)#end SW1#reload SW1(config)#interface vlan 1 SW1(config-if) #ipv6 address 2001:db8:acad:1::2/64 SW1(config-if)#no shutdown
Configure assigned IPv6 link-local address on PCA	IPv6 address:2001:db8:acad:1::3/64 Gateway:2001:db8: acad:1::1
Configure assigned IPv6 link-local address on PCB	IPv6 address:2001:db8: acad:1::4/64 Gateway:2001:db8: acad:1::1
To verify the configuration of the Router and/or Switch	R1#show ipv6 route SW1#show ipv6 route

To make the LLAs more recognizable as belonging to router R1, they are statically configured. The router R1 in this example has all of its interface configured with an LLA starting with fe80::n:1 where n is the network to which SW1, PCA, and PCB belong.

2.3 Dynamic Global Unicast Address Configuration (GUA)

Most devices typically receive IPv6 GUAs dynamically. A key IPv6 protocol suite called Neighbor Discovery Protocol (NDP) is what sends out RA (Router Advertisement) and RS (Router Solicitation) packets. Let's try to comprehend these messages and the role they play in locating and configuring IPv6 addresses in a network.

i. **Router Solicitation (RS) Message**

Purpose: The RS message is sent by an IPv6 host to inquire about the presence of routers on the local network. When a host is connected to an IPv6 network and needs to configure its IPv6 address, it can send an RS message to request router information.

Transmission: Hosts may send RS messages when they initially connect to the network or when they need to refresh their router information.

Multicast Address: The all-routers multicast address, ff02::2, is where RS messages are normally sent.

ii. **Router Advertisement (RA) Message**

Purpose: Routers can send the RA message in response to RS messages or regularly to educate hosts about their network settings and to broadcast their existence. Through RA messages, routers exchange data about the local network prefix, the default gateway, and various flags for address setting.

Transmission: Routers notify hosts of changes to the network configuration either periodically or in response to RS messages by sending them RA messages.

Multicast Address: The all-nodes multicast address, ff02::1, is the destination for RA transmissions.

iii. **Address Configuration**

When hosts receive RA messages, they configure their IPv6 addresses using the information contained in the RA messages. Hosts use their interface identifier in conjunction with the prefix information from the RA message to create a complete IPv6 address.

iv. **Managed and Stateless Address Configuration**

RA messages can specify whether hosts should get addresses using DHCPv6 (Managed Address Configuration) or stateless address autoconfiguration (SLAAC). This gives the network's address assignment and configuration flexibility.

In conclusion, RS and RA messages are essential parts of setting up an IPv6 address. Hosts can locate routers with the aid of RS messages, and routers can furnish hosts with crucial information to set up IPv6 addresses and network specifications through RA messages.

2.3.1 Router Advertisement Message Techniques

i. **SLAAC (Stateless Address Autoconfiguration)**

A device can generate its own GUA using SLAAC, eliminating the need for DHCPv6 services. When using SLAAC, devices rely on the local router's ICMPv6 RA messages to receive the required data. By default, the RA message advises the recipient device to generate its own IPv6 GUA and any other required information using the data in the RA message. A DHCPv6 server's services are not necessary. Since SLAAC lacks a central server (like a stateful DHCPv6 server) to assign GUAs and maintain a list of devices and their addresses, it is stateless. With SLAAC, the client device generates its own GUA based on the data in the RA message.

The two components of the address are constructed as follows, as the graphic illustrates:

i. Prefix - RA message advertises the prefix.

ii. Interface ID - Depending on the operating system of the device, either the EUI-64 procedure or a random 64-bit number generation is used.

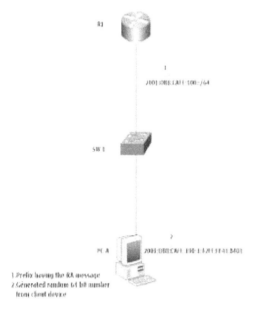

Step 1: The local link prefix is included in the RA message that the router transmits.

Step 2: The PC generates its interface ID and utilizes SLAAC to extract a prefix from the RA message.

ii. SLAAC and Stateless DHCPv6

SLAAC and stateless DHCPv6 can be set up on a router interface to deliver a router advertisement.

Devices perform the following courtesy of RA message:

- SLAAC creates its own unique IPv6 GUA.

- The router's LLA becomes the default gateway address, which is the RA source IPv6 address.

- A stateless DHCPv6 server gets additional data, like a domain name and DNS server address

Note: Domain names and DNS server addresses are distributed by a stateless DHCPv6 server. It doesn't distribute GUAs.

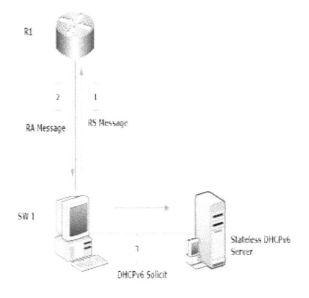

Step 1: The PC sends an RS to all IPv6 routers, "I need addressing information."

Step 2: All IPv6 nodes receive an RA message from the router specifying SLAAC and DHCPv6.This contains the details of your default gateway, prefix, and prefix-
length. However, a DHCPv6 server will need to provide you with DNS information.

Step 3: For a given DHCPv6 server, the PC sends a Solicit DHCPv6 packet. "I used **SLAAC** to create my IPv6 address and get my default gateway address, but I need other information from a stateless DHCPv6 server."

The type of device that gets a given IPv6 address is determined by a stateful DHCPv6 server, which also keeps track of information. For IPv4, DHCP is stateful.

Note: Only the RA message can be used to dynamically obtain the default gateway address. The default gateway address is not provided by the stateful or stateless DHCPv6 server

iii. **EUI-64 (Extended Unique Identifier-64)**

The process of automatically creating a unique interface identifier for a network interface in IPv6 addressing is known as EUI-64 (Extended Unique Identifier-64). Networked devices' IPv6 addresses are commonly configured via Stateless Address Autoconfiguration (SLAAC). The main uses of the EUI-64 process are global unicast addresses and link-local addresses.

Case study

The EUI-64 process will be carried out in the following manner, assuming that the router's interface mac address is 0001.4241.8401 and that the prefix for the global unicast address is 2001:0DB8: CAFE:0100::/64.

- **MAC Address Formation**

  The EUI-64 process starts with the 48-bit MAC address assigned to a network interface card (NIC).

  Hexadecimal notation is commonly used to express MAC addresses; in this example, 0001.4241.8401

- **Splitting the MAC Address**

  The MAC address which is a 48-bit-address is split into two equal parts: The two parts are the Organizationally Unique Identifier (OUI) and the Network Interface Card (NIC) specific part.

  The OUI is the first 24 bits (0001.42), and the NIC-specific part is the remaining 24 bits (41.8401).

- **Inserting FF: FE**

  "FF: FE," a 16-bit identification, is placed in between the OUI and the NIC-specific portion as follows:

  0001.42FFFE41.8401

  Align it into four hexadecimal digits

  0001:42FF: FE41:8401

- **Set the Universal/Local (U/L) Bit**

  The U/L (Universal/Local) bit is the seventh bit in the resulting EUI-64 Global Unicast Address.

  Convert the first two hexadecimal digits to binary as a nibble.

  In decimal it is   00

  In binary, it will be 00000000

  Invert the 7th bit

  00000010

  Convert to decimal

  0 2

  Attach it to the interface ID

  0201:42FF: FE41:8401

- **Construct the Global unicast address**

  Align the interface ID to the global routing prefix with the subnet ID

  2001:0DB8: CAFE: 0100:0201:42FF: FE41:8401

  Omit leading zeros if any to get the ipv6 address of a given interface or host.

  2001:DB8: CAFE: 100:201:42FF: FE41:8401

Since the MAC address and the "FF:FE" insertion combine to form a 64-bit identification, the resulting EUI-64 ensures uniqueness inside a network.

This procedure is frequently used in SLAAC for the automatic configuration of IPv6 addresses on a local network without the requirement for a DHCPv6 server.

EUI Configuration using a Router's Interface

Description	Command
Get into the interface configuration mode of R1.	R1(config) interface g0/0/0
Enable IPv6 unicast Routing and configure IPv6 address using Global unicast address prefix.	R1(config)#ipv6 unicast-routing R1(config)#int g0/0/0 R1(config-if) #ipv6 add 2001:DB8: CAFE: 100: :/64 eui-64 R1(config-if) #no shutdown
Verify the configuration of the IPv6 address for both Prefix and Interface ID	R1#show ipv6 interface brief GigabitEthernet0/0/0 [up/up] FE80::201:42FF: FE41:8401 {Link local address} 2001:DB8: CAFE: 100:201:42FF: FE41:8401 {Global unicast address}

Chapter 3: IPv6 Routing

IPv6 routing, which offers improved capabilities and addresses the shortcomings of its predecessor, IPv4, is the foundation of the next-generation Internet Protocol. With the increasing number of connected devices, IPv6 routing is becoming essential to the management of the digital environment. IPv6 routing enables scalable and effective communication due to its enhanced header structure, expanded address space, and streamlined packet processing.

Data transmission is made reliable and efficient by routing protocols, which allow routers to dynamically update their routing tables in response to changes in network topology.

Let's look at some of the key IPv6 routing protocols

3.1 Static Routing

In IPv6, network managers can manually configure routers with routing information that specifies the pathways for IPv6 traffic using a technique called static routing. In contrast to dynamic routing protocols, which use information exchanged between routers to update routing tables automatically, static routing requires a planned definition of routes. Static routing can be useful in smaller networks or for particular cases where simplicity and predictability are required, even though dynamic routing protocols are frequently more scalable and responsive to network changes.

These are the main features of IPv6 static routing.

Manual Configuration

In the case of static routing, router configuration data is manually input by network administrators. The next-hop router or exit interface, as well as the destination IPv6 network, must be specified.

Network Topology Considerations

In smaller networks with a generally stable topology and little to no change, static routing is frequently used. The overhead of maintaining static routes to reflect changes in topology might impede larger, more dynamic networks.

Predictability

Routing decisions can be clearly and consistently controlled with static routes. Network administration and troubleshooting are made easier for network administrators by their comprehensive understanding of traffic routing.

Resource Efficiency

Static routing requires fewer resources from routers than dynamic routing protocols because it eliminates the requirement for routers to engage in the sharing of routing information with one another. In situations with limited resources, this could be advantageous.

Routing Table Maintenance

If there are modifications to the network architecture, including adding or deleting routers or subnets, administrators must manually update static routes. Large, dynamic networks with plenty of changes can have this as a disadvantage.

Security Considerations

In certain situations, static routing can improve security by lowering the attack surface connected to dynamic routing protocols. Malicious actors have fewer options for creating bogus routing information because static routes are explicitly established.

Types Static Routing

The following are the types of IPv6 static routes similar to IPv4.

i. **Standard static route**

A standard static route is a form of static routing configuration that is commonly used in computer networks. It entails setting a single static route for all traffic destined for a certain network or server manually. The network administrator defines the following parameters in a standard static route:

- **Host or Destination Network**: This is the network address or IPv6 address of the destination host to which data packets should be delivered.

- **Next-Hop Address**: The IPv6 address of the next device (router) on the way to the destination is the next-hop address. It acts as the gateway through which data packets should be sent to their destination.

- **Outgoing Interface**: Some setups allow you to provide the outgoing interface directly instead of the next-hop IPv6 address. The router will utilize its routing table to choose the appropriate next hop in this case.

When a data packet arrives at a router, it compares the destination IPv6 address to the static routes that have been established. If the destination IPv6 address matches any of the static routes, the router forwards the packet using the information in the static route configuration. If no match is found in the static routes, the router will attempt to find a route using alternative methods, such as dynamic routing protocols or a default route.

ii. Default static route

A "default route" is a special setting in the network configuration of a router that determines the path to take when no specified route is available for a certain destination IPv6 address. It acts as a default gateway, allowing data to be sent to other networks or the internet when the device lacks a more specified route to a specific destination. It essentially functions as a "catch-all" route, guaranteeing that data can be transferred even when the destination is not expressly known to the device.

Sure, let's take an example to clarify the concept of a default route: Assume you are a delivery driver for a corporation that delivers packages to various residences in a town. You have a list of precise addresses (routes) to which you must deliver packages. You organize your itinerary accordingly, visiting each address depending on the information you have.

However, one day your employer sends you a package bearing an address you've never seen before and that isn't on your list. You have no idea where to distribute it because you have no explicit instructions for that place.

In this case:

The routing table of a network device, such as a router or a computer, is represented by the delivery list with specific addresses. The known addresses on the list are specific routes in the routing table that tell the device where to forward data to specified destinations.

The package with the strange address contains inbound data that the gadget must send to a place it has never encountered before.

The "**default route**" now comes into play:

Your supervisor provides you with the following default instruction: "If you don't know where to deliver a package, just drop it off at the main post office."

The main post office operates as the "default gateway" for your delivery in this scenario. If you can't find the address on your list (special route), you always have the option of taking the item to the main post office (default route) for additional handling and delivery. The default route serves as a safety net, ensuring that data can still be delivered even if the destination is unknown or not defined in the routing table.

iii. **Floating static route**

A "floating static route" is a routing arrangement in which a static route is assigned a greater administrative distance or metric than another route. This technique is widely used to construct a backup route that becomes active only when the primary route fails.

Routing tables are used by routers to determine the best path for data packets to take to their destinations. A static route is a routing table item that has been manually set to specify the path to a single target network. However, in some cases, having a backup route that takes effect when the primary route fails may be useful.

That's where the concept of a floating static route comes in:

Assume you own a small firm with two internet service providers (ISPs) providing internet access to your location. You want to make sure that your network stays connected to the internet even if one of the ISPs goes down. You decide to create a floating static route to do this.

In this scenario:

Principal Route (Higher Priority): ISP A is your principal internet provider, and its connection is quicker and more dependable. In your router, you set up a static route that directs all outgoing internet traffic to ISP A's gateway.

Backup Route (Lower Priority): ISP B is your secondary internet provider, and it acts as a backup if ISP A fails. You install another static route in your router that directs all outgoing internet traffic to ISP B's gateway, but this route has a greater administrative distance or metric. The higher the administrative distance, the less desirable it is for it to be the preferred route.

Let's take a look at how the floating static route works:

Normally, your router will use the primary route with ISP A (the one with the shortest administrative distance) to forward all data packets to the internet. This path is recommended since it has a higher metric, resulting in faster and more efficient data transmission. However, if ISP A goes down or becomes unreachable, your router will notice the problem. Because the primary route is no longer available, the router will switch to the backup route with ISP B (higher administrative distance). This floating static route becomes active, allowing your workplace network to maintain internet connectivity through the backup ISP.

Network managers can improve network resiliency and redundancy by installing floating static routes, guaranteeing that data can still be sent to its destination even if the primary route fails. This strategy improves network resilience and reduces downtime, which is critical for businesses that rely significantly on internet connection for day-to-day operations.

Next-Hop Option Concept

The next hop in a static route can be indicated by an IPv6 address, an exit interface, or both.

The way the destination is supplied results in one of three types of static routes:

i. **Next-hop path**- Only the IPv6 address of the following hop is supplied.

ii. **The static route that is directly connected to** the router exit interface is the only one listed.

iii. **Completely stated static route-** The IPv6 address of the next hop and the exit interface are supplied.

Standard Static Route Configuration using Next-hop-path option

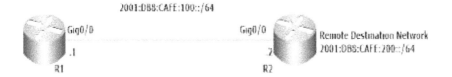

Assumptions

Destination IPv6 network: 2001:DB8: CAFE:200: :/64

IPv6 address next-hop router:2001:DB8: CAFÉ:100::2

Description	Command
Get into the router's global configuration mode	R1(config)#
Specify the IPv6 route command followed by the destination network address and its prefix and finally the IPv6 address of the neighbor router also known as the next hop	R1(config)#IPv6 route 2001:DB8: CAFÉ:200: :/64 2001:DB8: CAFÉ:100::2

Return to Privileged Exec mode	R1(config)#end
Saves the configuration to the router's NVRAM, to ensure that the static route remains in place after a reboot.	R1#copy running-config startup-config
Verify your configuration	R1#show ipv6 route R1#show ipv6 interface brief

Default static Route Configuration

2001:DB8:CAFE:100::/64

Gig0/0 .1   R1

Gig0/0 .2   R2

Current Router's Interface

Next-Hop Router

Assumptions:

IPv6 address of the current router's interface: 2001:DB8: CAFÉ:100::1

IPv6 address of the next hop router: 2001:DB8: CAFÉ:100::2

Description	Command
Get into the router's global configuration mode	R1(config)#
To match any network address, use the IPv6 route	R1(config)#IPv6 route::/0 2001:DB8: CAFÉ:100::2

command with::/0 to represent the default route and specify the next hop address.	
Return to Privileged Exec mode	R1(config)#end
Saves the configuration to the router's NVRAM, to ensure that the static route remains in place after a reboot.	R1#copy running-config startup-config
Verify your configuration	R1#show ipv6 route R1#show ipv6 interface brief

The command IPv6 route::/0 informs the router that any communication destined for a network location other than its own should be routed to the designated next-hop router.

Floating static Route Configuration

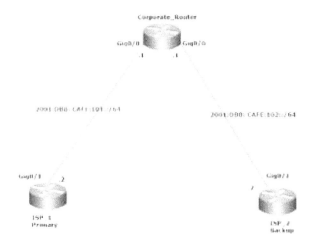

Assumptions:

Router IPv6 address: 2001:DB8: CAFÉ:101::1

Primary next-hop gateway: 2001:DB8: CAFÉ:101::2

Backup next-hop gateway: 2001:DB8: CAFÉ:102::2

Administrative distance for the backup route: 10

DescrIPv6tion	Command
Get into the router's global configuration mode	Corporate_Router(config)#
Add a major static route by instructing the router to forward all traffic with a destination not specific (::/0)to the main next-hop	Corporate_Router (config)# ipv6 route ::/0 2001:DB8:CAFE:101::2

gateway address 2001:DB8: CAFÉ:101::2	
Add a floating static route (backup route) by instructing the router to send all incoming traffic with no specified destination (::/0)to the backup next-hop gateway at IPv6 address 2001:DB8: CAFÉ:102::2 but with a greater administrative distance of 10	Corporate_Router (config)# ipv6 route ::/0 2001:DB8:CAFE:102::2 10
Return to Privileged Exec mode	Corporate_Router (config)#end
Saves the configuration to the router's NVRAM, to ensure that the static route remains in place after a reboot.	Corporate_Router #copy running-config startup-config
Verify your configuration	Corporate_Router #show ipv6 route Corporate_Router #show ipv6 interface brief

A floating static route indicates that the backup route will only be employed if the primary route fails or becomes inaccessible.

With static routing, network managers can easily configure routing tables on devices manually the paths that data should follow across networks. Static routing, as opposed to dynamic routing technologies, uses explicit, predefined route entries to direct traffic flow inside a network. Smaller networks with stable topologies can benefit from this strategy's simplicity, predictability, and resource efficiency. Static routing gives you precise control over routing choices, but it may not scale well in large-scale or dynamic applications and requires manual updates for changes in network architecture. Static routing is still useful, despite its drawbacks, in situations where resource efficiency and simplicity of setup are important considerations.

3.2 Routing Information Protocol next generation (RIPng)

The Routing Information Protocol Next Generation (RIPng) is an IPv6-specific modification of the original Routing Information Protocol (RIP). This distance-vector routing technique works well with networks that range in size from small to medium. RIPng functions on the network layer (Layer 3) of the OSI model and employs a distance-vector routing algorithm, just like its IPv4 equivalent. Larger networks may find that RIPng is slower or less scalable than other protocols, despite its ease of configuration and management.

Features and characteristics of RIPng

IPv6 Support

RIPng is designed specifically for IPv6 networks enabling routers to communicate routing information using IPv6 addresses.

Distance-Vector Routing Algorithm

To find the best path to a destination network, RIPng employs a distance-vector routing algorithm. Every router periodically notifies its neighbors about its routing table

Hop Count Metric

The RIPng metric is hop count. The most important component in choosing the optimal route is the number of routers, or hops, that separate the source and destination.

Split Horizon and Route Poisoning

To avoid routing loops, RIPng uses strategies like split horizon and route poisoning. Route poisoning designates inaccessible routes with an endless metric, whereas split horizon stops a router from advertising routes back onto the interface from whence they were learned.

Periodic Updates

To keep their nearby routers informed about their routing tables, RIPng routers send updates to them regularly. Routers can keep an accurate picture of the network topology with the support of these updates.

Limited Scalability

Although RIPng is easy to set up, its scalability is not as great as that of more complex routing protocols, such as OSPFv3 (Open Shortest Path First version 3) or IPv6's EIGRP. For big, dynamic networks, it might not be the ideal option.

Convergence Time

RIPng convergence time, when measured against other routing protocols, can be comparatively slow, meaning that it takes longer for routers to update their routing tables following a topology change. This may be problematic in networks when quick convergence is essential.

Compatibility

RIP for IPv4 is not backward compatible with RIPng. When a network has routers for both IPv4 and IPv6, IPv6 should utilize RIPng, whereas IPv4 should use RIP (IPv4).

RIPng Configuration

When two or more routers are configured with RIPng (Routing Information Protocol for IPv6), they communicate with one another to discover IPv6 routes in each other's networks. As a dynamic protocol it enables routers to exchange and update routing tables, giving them the information, they need to decide which routes are the most efficient for reaching various IPv6 destinations.

Loopback 1

2001:DB8:CAFE:101::/64

2001:DB8:CAFE:100::/64

G0:0/0   G0:0/0

Loopback 1

2001:DB8:CAFE:102::/64

(Interfaces are generated using EUI)

Let's consider a scenario where we need to configure RIPng on two routers (Router X and Router Y) for IPv6 routing. These routers are directly connected through a shared network with the following IPv6 address and Interfaces.

Router X

Directly connected GigabitEthernet 0/0/0:

2001:DB8:CAFE:100:230:A3FF:FEB8:BE01

Interface-Loopback 1:

2001:DB8:CAFE:101:201:64FF:FE8A:A03E

Router Y

Directly connected Gigabit Ethernet 0/0/0:

2001:DB8:CAFE:100:202:4AFF:FE34:2501

Interface-Loopback 1:

2001:DB8:CAFE:102:2E0:A3FF:FEEC:A76

Note: The above interface addresses were generated using the Extended unique Identifier method.

Description	Command

On Router X enter into global configuration command and enable the forwarding of IPv6 unicast traffic.	RX(config)# ipv6 unicast-routing
Enable RIPng on the router with a selected string to identify the process in this case "XYZ" and get into RIPng configuration mode.	RX(config)# ipv6 router rip XYZ
Enable the IPv6 routing process on a specified interface i.e. gig0/0/0 and Loopback interface using the identity process string.	RX (config-rtr)#interface loopback 1 RX (config-if)#ipv6 rip XYZ enable RX (config-if)#interface gig0/0/0 RX (config-if)#ipv6 rip XYZ enable RX (config-if)#end RX #
Save your configuration on Router X	RX #write Building configuration... [OK]
On Router Y enter into global configuration command and enable the forwarding of IPv6 unicast traffic.	RY(config)# ipv6 unicast-routing
Enable RIPng on the router with a selected string to identify the	RY(config)# ipv6 router rip XYZ

process in this case "XYZ" and get into RIPng configuration mode. It should be the same compared to the RX	
Enable the IPv6 routing process on a specified interface i.e. gig0/0/0 and Loopback interface using the identity process string.	RY (config-rtr)#interface loopback 1 RY (config-if)#ipv6 rip XYZ enable RY (config-if)#interface gig0/0/0 RY (config-if)#ipv6 rip XYZ enable RY (config-if)#end RY #
Save your configuration on Router Y	RY #write Building configuration... [OK]
To view networks remotely learned.	RX# show ipv6 route RY# show ipv6 route

The main difference between IPv6 RIPng configuration and RIPv2 for IPv4 is the decision to define interfaces directly instead of utilizing network addresses. RIPng (Routing Information Protocol for IPv6) is frequently configured on individual interfaces rather than through network addresses. The advantages and considerations and Considerations of this approach.

Advantages

   i. **Simplicity**

The configuration procedure is made simpler by configuring RIPng directly on interfaces. Just enable RIPng on the interfaces that take part in the routing operation; no network declarations are required

ii. **Automatic Interface Inclusion**

The connected networks to an interface are automatically included in the routing process when RIPng is enabled on that interface. Dynamic inclusion can make configuration duties easier, particularly in situations where networks may change.

iii. **Ease of Understanding**

It becomes easier to configure, especially when we get to use other IPv6 routing protocols like OSPFv3. Enabling routing on individual links instead of summarizing networks is consistent with the idea of turning on RIPng directly on interfaces.

Considerations

i. **Interface Changes Impact Routing**

An interface that has RIPng enabled will be affected by any changes made to it, including the addition or removal of IP addresses. Knowing which interfaces are taking part in RIPng and which networks they are connected to is important.

ii. **Lack of Fine-Grained Control**

Unlike RIPv2 for IPv4, where network statements can be used to select which networks to include, RIPng configured on interfaces may lack fine-grained control. If you need more control over which networks are advertised, you may need to use another routing technology or a combination of static routes and RIPng.

iii. **Automatic Summarization**

RIPng employs automatic summarization at network boundaries, which can result in inadequate routing in certain instances. This behavior should be evaluated if precise control over subnet advertisement is needed.

In summary, the choice to employ interface-specific configuration in IPv6 RIPng is based on the specific needs and preferences of the network administrator. It's a reasonable strategy, especially for simpler designs of networks, but in more complex cases, meticulous consideration of its implications is essential.

3.3 Enhanced Interior Gateway Routing Protocol for IPv6 (EIGRPv6)

EIGRPv6, or Enhanced Interior Gateway Routing Protocol for IPv6, is a complex routing protocol designed to provide efficient and scalable communication within IPv6 networks. EIGRPv6 is a protocol developed by Cisco Systems that expands on the success of IPv4 by integrating changes to handle the specific characteristics of the IPv6 addressing scheme. EIGRPv6 retains its core features, such as rapid convergence, loop-free operation, and support for variable-length subnet masking, while also introducing advancements tailored to IPv6 specifics, such as simplified configuration through link-local addresses and integration of multicast communication. This protocol is renowned for its ability to adapt to network changes dynamically, providing a resilient and scalable solution for routing in modern IPv6 environments.

EIGRPv6 Inter-Router Communication

Routed Protocols IPv4 and IPv6 use a well-known protocol ID of 88 to identify EIGRP packets.

When EIGRPv6 is enabled, the IPv6 link-local address of the interface is used as the source for communication between the routers. The multicast link-local address FF02::A or a unicast link-local address may be the destination address.

The source and destination addresses for each type of EIGRP packet are displayed in the table below.

EIGRP Packet	Source	Destination	Purpose
Hello	Link-local address	FF02::A	Neighbor discovery and keepalive
Acknowledgment	Link-local address	Link-local address	Acknowledges receipt of an update
Query	Link-local address	FF02::A	Request for route information during a topology change event

Reply	Link-local address	Link-local address	A response to a query Message.
Update	Link-local address	Link-local address	Adjacency forming
Update	Link-local address	FF02::A	Topology change

EIGRPv6 Configuration

IPv6 on EIGRP can be enabled through the original IOS approach, known as classic mode. An autonomous system number is used in this mode to configure the routing process.

The following are the procedures to configure EIGRPv6 on an IOS router:

Step 1: Use the global configuration command to configure EIGRPv6 using ipv6 router eigrp as-number.

Step 2: Use the IPv6 address family command eigrp router-id id to assign the router ID. To ensure effective routing process operation, the router ID should be explicitly assigned. EIGRP's default approach is to assign a router ID locally based on the highest IPv4 loopback address or, if that is not available, the highest IPv4 address.

Step 3: Use the command ipv6 eigrp as-number as an interface parameter to enable the procedure on the interface.

Let's consider a scenario where we need to configure EIGRPv6 on two routers (Router X and Router Y) for IPv6 routing. These routers are directly

{Interfaces are generated using EUI}

connected through a shared network with the following IPv6 address and Interfaces.

Router X

Directly connected GigabitEthernet 0/0/0:

2001:DB8:CAFE:100:2E0:A3FF:FE3A:8C01

Interface-Loopback 1:

2001:DB8:CAFE:101:230:A3FF:FE71:1038

Router Y

Directly connected Gigabit Ethernet 0/0/0:

2001:DB8:CAFE:100:205:5EFF:FE7C:C701

Interface-Loopback 1:

2001:DB8:CAFE:102:20C:CFFF:FE66:CCA5

Note: The above interface addresses were generated using the Extended unique Identifier method

Description	Command
On Router X enter into global configuration command and enable the forwarding of	RX(config)# ipv6 unicast-routing

IPv6 unicast traffic.	
Enable EIGRPv6 on the router using appropriate AS_No between (1-65535). In this case, we shall use 100.	RX(config)# ipv6 router eigrp 100
Now set a unique identifier for the router within the EIGRP routing domain known as router-id. In this let's use 1.1.1.1 instead of the local IPv4 loopback/Actual IPv4 address. Activate the router's interface to enable the EIGRP routing process by issuing the command no shutdown.	RX(config-rtr)#eigrp router-id 1.1.1.1 RX(config-rtr)#no shutdown
Enter into the interface configuration mode of the Loopback and	RX(config)#interface Loopback 1 RX(config-if) #ipv6 eigrp 100

GigabitEthernet 0/0/0. This applies to any other interface available on the router. Turn on EIGRPv6 on the designated interface, then link it to the EIGRP AS number-in this example, 100.	RX (config-if) #interface g0/0/0 RX(config-if) #ipv6 eigrp 100
Save your configuration on Router X	RX #write Building configuration... [OK]
On Router Y enter into global configuration command and enable the forwarding of IPv6 unicast traffic.	RY(config)# ipv6 unicast-routing
Enable EIGRPv6 on the router using appropriate AS_No between (1-65535). Use the same AS Number.	RY(config)# ipv6 router eigrp 100

Now set a unique identifier for the router within the EIGRP routing domain known as router id. In this let's use 1.1.1.1 instead of the local IPv4 loopback/Actual IPv4 address. Activate the router's interface to enable EIGRP routing process by issuing the command no shutdown.	RY(config-rtr)#eigrp router-id 1.1.1.1 RY(config-rtr)#no shutdown
Enter into the interface configuration mode of the Loopback and GigabitEthernet 0/0/0.This applies to any other interface available on the router. Turn on EIGRPv6 on the designated interface, then link	RY(config)#interface Loopback 1 RY(config-if) #ipv6 eigrp 100 RY (config-if) #interface g0/0/0 RY(config-if) #ipv6 eigrp 100

it to the EIGRP AS number-in this example, 100.	
Save your configuration on Router Y	RY #write Building configuration... [OK]
To view networks remotely learned.	RX# show ipv6 route RY# show ipv6 route
To view the current state of the active routing protocol process	RX# show ipv6 protocols RY# show ipv6 protocols

All IPv6-enabled interfaces begin routing immediately once the IPv6 address family is set up for the EIGRP-named process.

Split Horizon

This is a loop-prevention feature that stops a router from advertising routes that were learned on the same interface.

The show ipv6 eigrp interfaces detail command can be used by a network administrator to determine whether the split horizon is active or disabled.

Split horizon is a problem in EIGRPv6 network designs that require routes to be advertised out of the interfaces from which they were learned either a nonbroadcast multi-access (NBMA) Frame Relay hub-and-spoke topology or a Dynamic Multipoint Virtual Private Network (DMVPN) network, both of which use multipoint interfaces on the hub. In these networks, the hub must be configured to disable split horizon.

EIGRPv6 is distinguished by its efficiency, scalability, and capacity to adapt dynamically to network changes. It offers greater flexibility and administrative simplicity. Overall, EIGRPv6 provides a strong and adaptive routing system for the ever-changing IPv6 network landscape.

3.4 Open Shortest Path First for IPv6 (OSPFv3)

The Open Shortest Path First for IPv6 (OSPFv3) routing protocol is normally used by IPv6 networks to enable efficient and scalable routing. OSPFv3 protocol brought the stable and well-known features of the IPv4 OSPF protocol to the IPv6 environment. It's a link-state routing protocol that shares information about network topology to find the shortest paths between destinations. Several IPv6 address families are supported, and they can function in point-to-point, broadcast, and non-broadcast networks. It can also establish neighbor connections to exchange routing information. Network management is simplified by employing link-local addresses. Effective scaling in big networks is made possible by the hierarchical structure. Setting up interfaces, allocating spaces, and setting OSPFv3 processes are all part of the configuration. When it comes to dynamic routing in IPv6 networks, OSPFv3 is a solid and scalable option that guarantees efficient communication and adaptability to network changes.

OSPFv3 Communication

OSPFv3 packets use protocol ID 89, and routers communicate with each other using the local interface's IPv6 link-local address as the source. Depending on the packet type, the destination address is either a unicast link-local address or a multicast link-local scoped address

FF02::05: OSPFv3 AllSPFRouters

FF02::06: OSPFv3 AllDRouters designated router (DR) router

Packet types for OSPFv3

Typ e	Packet Name	Source	Destination	Purpose
1.	Hello	Link-local address	FF02::5(all routers)	Discover and maintain neighbors
		Link-local address	Link-local address	Initial adjacency forming, immediate hello
2	Database description	Link-local address	Link-local address	Summarize database contents
3	Link state request	Link-local address	Link-local address	Database information request
4	Link state update	Link-local address	Link-local address	Initial adjacency forming, in response to link state request
		Link-local address (from DR)	FF02::5(all routers)	Database update
		Link-local address(from non-DR)	FF02::6(DR/BDR)	Database update
5	Link state acknowledgment	Link-local address	Link-local address	Initial adjacency forming, in response to link state update

		Link-local address (from DR)	FF02::5(all routers)	Flooding acknowledgeme nt
		Link-local address (from non-DR)	FF02::6(DR/BD R)	Flooding acknowledgeme nt

OSPFv3 Configuration

To enable the routing protocol on routers and specify its parameters, OSPFv3 configuration requires the following steps:

Step 1. Start the routing process by configuring OSPFv3 with the command router ospfv3[process-id], after turning on IPv6 unicast routing on the router.

Step 2:To define the router ID (RID), use the router-id command. The router ID is a 32-bit number that does not have to match an IPv4 address. As long as the value is distinct within the OSPF domain, it can be any integer. The method used by OSPFv3 and OSPFv2 to dynamically locate the RID is the same.

Step 3: Use the optional address-family {ipv6 | ipv4} unicast command to initialize the address-family within the routing procedure. When OSPFv3 is turned on for an interface, the relevant address family gets turned on automatically.

Step 4: To enable the protocol and assign the interface to an area, use the interface command ospfv3 process-id ipv6 area area-id

Let's consider a scenario where we need to configure OSPFv3 on two routers running on the backbone area(0) (Router X and Router Y) for IPv6 routing. These routers are directly connected through a shared network with the following IPv6 address and Interfaces.

Router X

Directly connected Gigabit Ethernet 0/0/0:

2001:DB8:CAFE:100:2E0:A3FF:FE3A:8C01

Interface-Loopback 1:

2001:DB8:CAFE:101:230:A3FF:FE71:1038

Router Y

Directly connected Gigabit Ethernet 0/0/0:

2001:DB8:CAFE:100:205:5EFF:FE7C:C701

Interface-Loopback 1:

2001:DB8:CAFE:102:20C:CFFF:FE66:CCA5

Note: The above interface addresses were generated using the Extended unique Identifier method

Description	Command
On Router X enter into global configuration command and enable the forwarding of IPv6 unicast traffic.	RX(config)# ipv6 unicast-routing
Set up OSPFv3 on RX and provide the process ID (600 is used in this example, although there are more options available to choose from 1-65535). Process ID is used to distinguish between	RX(config)# ipv6 router ospf 600

different OSPF processes that may be running on the same router and are locally meaningful.	
Next, configure OSPFv3 to use the IPv4 address as the router ID, we shall use 1.1.1.1 a 32-bit number that does not necessarily have to match an IPv4 address. Within the OSPF autonomous system (AS), the router ID serves as a unique identification for	RX(config-rtr)# router-id 1.1.1.1

the OSPFv3 router.	
Configure OSPFv3 on a specified interface in this case Loopback 1 and Gig0/0/0 with the process ID 600. Specify the area where the interface belongs to. For this configuration, it belongs to the backbone area (area 0).	RX(config)#interface Loopback 1 RX(config-if) # ipv6 ospf 600 area 0 RX (config-if) #interface g0/0/0 RX(config-if) # ipv6 ospf 600 area 0
Save your configuration on Router X	RX #write Building configuration... [OK]
On Router Y enter into global configuration	RY(config)# ipv6 unicast-routing

command and enable the forwarding of IPv6 unicast traffic.	
Set up OSPFv3 on RX and provide the process ID (600 is used in this example, although there are more options available to choose from 1-65535). Process ID is used to distinguish between different OSPF processes that may be running on the same	RY(config)# ipv6 router ospf 600

router and are locally meaningful.	
Next, configure OSPFv3 to use the IPv4 address as the router ID, we shall use 1.1.1.1 a 32-bit number that does not necessarily have to match an IPv4 address. Within the OSPF autonomous system (AS), the router ID serves as a unique identification for the OSPFv3 router.	RY(config-rtr)# router-id 1.1.1.1
Configure OSPFv3 on a	RY(config)#interface Loopback 1

specified interface in this case Loopback 1 and Gig0/0/0 with the process ID 600. Specify the area where the interface belongs to. For this configuration, it belongs to the backbone area (area 0).	RY(config-if) # ipv6 ospf 600 area 0 RY (config-if) #interface g0/0/0 RY(config-if) # ipv6 ospf 600 area 0
Save your configuration on Router Y	RY #write Building configuration... [OK]
To view networks remotely learned.	RX# show ipv6 route RY# show ipv6 route
To view the current state of the active routing protocol process	RX# show ipv6 protocols RY# show ipv6 protocols

In conclusion, OSPFv3 is a dependable and scalable routing protocol made for IPv6 networks that enables efficient and reliable routing information sharing to support communication inside complex network architectures.

Chapter 4: IPv6 Transition Mechanisms

With IPv4 addresses running out and IPv6 offering seamless possibilities, it is critical to introduce IPv6 transition methods in the dynamic world of networking. We will explore the key strategies and systems that allow IPv4 and IPv6 to coexist and provide a seamless transition for enterprises going through the tricky landscape of IP protocol evolution.

This topic aspires to enable the reader a thorough understanding of the tools available to them, ranging from creative tunneling approaches to dual-stack implementations that bridge the old and the new. Examine the details of the IPv6 transition, talk about security issues, and acquire knowledge about how LAN, ISP, and mobile networks are deployed.

Building resilient, future-ready networks requires an understanding of these transition mechanisms, which is becoming more than just a need as the demand for IP addresses escalates.

The following mechanisms will help us figure out how to transition from all-IPv4 to a combination of IPv4 and IPv6(dual stack) and then to all-IPv6.

4.1 Dual-Stack Implementation

The term "dual stack" often refers to the simultaneous deployment of Internet Protocol version 4 (IPv4) and Internet Protocol version 6 (IPv6) on a network or device. IPv4 and IPv6 are the two primary versions of the Internet Protocol, which addresses and routes data packets across networks. IPv4 addresses have grown scarce as the demand for IP addresses has increased due to the expansion of the internet. IPv6 was created to help solve this scarcity by giving a significantly bigger address space. IPv4 is still widely used, and many networks and devices rely on it courtesy of a technology known as Network Address Translation (NAT).

By enabling dual stack, systems can handle both IPv4 and IPv6 protocols, facilitating an easy transition from IPv4 to IPv6 without resulting in connectivity issues. Given how the internet develops and how much demand there is for IP addresses, this shift is essential. Dual stack guarantees communication between devices and IPv4 and IPv6-enabled systems during the coexistence period.

Depending on the capabilities of the devices involved, IPv4 or IPv6 can be used for communication in a dual-stack environment. This strategy makes it easier to go from IPv4 to IPv6, enabling businesses and service providers to embrace the new protocol while maintaining compatibility with their current IPv4 infrastructure.

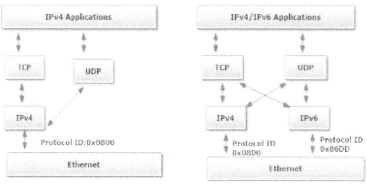

To process IPv4 and IPv6 packets, a dual-stack node needs to have functionality in the Internet Layer of its network stack. Sending and receiving IPv4 or IPv6 packets is often limited to a single Link Layer. The IPv6 Neighbor Discovery (ND) protocol and the IPv4 Address Resolution Protocol (ARP) are both contained in the Link Layer.

The Transport Layer handles IPv4 and IPv6 packets in almost the same way, except for one little difference: the checksum, which is derived from the IP header and includes the source and destination IP addresses, is computed differently for TCP and UDP. Invocations of the IPv4 socket API, IPv6 basic socket API, and IPv6 advanced socket API routines are possible from the Application Layer code. The IPv6 side of the IP Layer is accessible via IPv6 socket functions, whereas the IPv4 side is accessible through IPv4 socket functions.

The node should be able to configure the IPv4 network, which includes setting up a node address, default gateway, subnet mask, and DNS server addresses in 32-bit IPv4 addresses. You have three options for configuring this information: manually, through DHCPv4, or in a mix of both. The node should also be able to configure the IPv6 network, which includes setting up a default gateway, a link-local IP address, one or more global unicast addresses, the subnet length, and DNS server addresses, all of which are 128-bit IPv6 addresses.

This configuration data can be set up manually, automatically through DHCPv6, automatically through Stateless Address Autoconfiguration, or in any combination of these methods.

On a dual-stack node, IPv4-only and IPv6-only applications (client, server, and peer-to-peer) will function smoothly. They will only call functions on one side of the network stack when making system calls. The fact that they are operating on a dual-stack node does not give them any additional capability to accept or establish connections across the other IP version.8

4.2 Tunneling

The process of encapsulating one network protocol inside another is known as tunneling. Tunneling facilitates the transfer of IPv6 packets over IPv4 networks and vice versa. It gives networks that might not support the current version of the Internet Protocol a way to communicate with one another.

In the context of the IPv4 to IPv6 transition, the following are a few significant features of tunneling:

 i. **Types of Tunnels**

 IPv6 over IPv4 Tunneling (6in4): This type of tunnel encapsulates IPv6 packets within IPv4 packets. It is one of the most often utilized tunneling methods for IPv6 deployment over an existing IPv4 infrastructure.

IPv4 over IPv6 Tunneling (4in6): This is the opposite of 6in4, in which IPv4 packets are encapsulated within IPv6 packets. Although it is less common, it can be applied in some situations when IPv6 is the most widely used protocol.

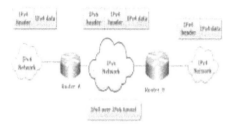

ii. **Automatic Tunneling**

6to4: This automatic tunneling method eliminates the need for manual configuration by enabling IPv6 communication across an IPv4 infrastructure. It embeds the IPv4 address into the IPv6 address using a unique IPv6 prefix (2002::/16).

iii. **Teredo Tunneling**

For devices hidden behind Network Address Translation (NAT) devices, Teredo is a tunneling protocol that enables IPv6 connection. It enables the tunneling of IPv6 packets through IPv4 and UDP (User Datagram Protocol).

iv. **Manual Tunneling**

Generic Routing Encapsulation (GRE) is one technology that
network managers can use to manually configure tunnels between
IPv4 and IPv6 networks.

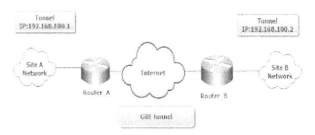

v. **Encapsulation and Decapsulation**

Encapsulation: When tunneling occurs, the original packet (IPv6 in 6in4
scenarios, or IPv4 in 4in6) is encapsulated in a new packet of the router
protocol (IPv4 or IPv6). This outer packet is used to transport the inside
packet over the network.

Decapsulation: The outer packet is removed upon arrival at the destination,
and the receiving system extracts and processes the inside packet.

vi. **Tunneling Challenges**

MTU (Maximum Transmission Unit) Issues: Tunneling
introduces a second layer to the packet, which could lead to issues
with MTU. It is necessary to establish path MTU discovery
procedures to prevent fragmentation problems.

Security Concerns: Network security becomes more challenging
when tunneling is used. Encrypted traffic must be secured, and
trusted tunnel endpoints must be established.

vii. **Deployment Scenarios**

Transitional Periods: When IPv4 and IPv6 coexist during transitional periods, tunneling is frequently used. It makes communication possible between networks that use various IP versions.

viii. **Transition Mechanism**

Coexistence Strategy: In addition to dual stack, tunneling is one of the transition techniques. It facilitates the seamless transition of enterprises from IPv4 to IPv6 while preserving network connectivity between IP versions.

In conclusion, tunneling is a flexible networking technology that may be applied to a variety of scenarios, such as the IPv4–IPv6 transition. It is essential for enabling smooth transitions between networks running multiple protocol versions, such as IPv4 and IPv6, and for facilitating communication across networks running different protocol versions.

4.3 NAT64 (Network Address Translation 64)

Network Address Translation 64 (NAT64) is a technology that allows devices to communicate using Internet Protocol version 6 (IPv6) and IPv4 (IPv4). As the entire world advances from IPv4 to IPv6, due to the exhaustion of accessible IPv4 addresses, mechanisms for communication between the two protocol versions are required. NAT64 accomplishes this by enabling IPv6-only and IPv4-only hosts to interact with one another.

The way NAT64 works

i. **IPv6-only Host**: An IPv6-only host makes a connection with an IPv4-only host or server.

ii. **DNS64:** Before initiating a connection, the IPv6-only host normally requests a DNS64 server. DNS64 converts IPv4 addresses into IPv6 addresses. It provides an IPv6 address for the requested IPv4 target.

iii. **NAT64 Gateway**: The IPv6-only host transmits packets to a NAT64 gateway, which is a device that translates IPv6 into IPv4. The NAT64 gateway uses both IPv6 and IPv4 addresses.

iv. **IPv6 to IPv4 Translation**: The NAT64 gateway receives the IPv6 packet from the IPv6-only host, modifies the packet headers, and wraps it as an IPv4 packet. This involves modifying the source IPv6 address to its own IPv6 address and translating the destination IPv6 address (obtained from DNS64) to the matching IPv4 address.

v. **IPv4 Network**: The encapsulated IPv4 packet is subsequently delivered over the IPv4 network and routed to the destination IPv4-only host.

vi. **IPv4 to IPv6 Translation**: When an IPv4 packet arrives at the destination IPv4-only host, the NAT64 gateway of the destination network executes the reverse translation. It retrieves the original IPv6 packet from the enclosed IPv4 packet, restores the IPv6 header, and sends it to the IPv6-only destination host.

NAT64 serves as a bridge between IPv6 and IPv4 networks, allowing devices with various IP versions to communicate with one another. DNS64 assists by assigning IPv6 addresses to IPv4-only hosts. This method facilitates the transition from IPv4 to IPv6, allowing communication across the two protocols.

NAT64 has two primary types: stateless and stateful. They describe how the NAT64 gateway handles the translation of IPv6 packets to IPv4. Let's look at the differences between them.

Stateless NAT64

i. **Basic Operation:** Stateless NAT64 does not store any mapping or state information for the translation. A stateless technique is used to translate each IPv6 address to its corresponding IPv4 address. The translation is entirely based on information contained in the IPv6 and IPv4 headers.

ii. **Scalability:** Stateless NAT64 is generally more scalable because it does not need to keep track of the status of each connection. Because it does not keep any state, it can effectively handle a huge number of concurrent connections.

iii. **Connection Independence**: Each IPv6-to-IPv4 translation operates independently of the others.
Stateless NAT64 processes each packet separately and ignores the context of earlier transmissions in the same connection.

iv. **Use Cases:** Stateless NAT64 is appropriate for situations where basic translation is sufficient and connection-specific information does not need to be tracked.

Stateful NAT64

i. **Maintaining State**: To create a mapping between IPv6 and IPv4 addresses for active connections, stateful NAT64 maintains track of the state for each translation.

Details like source and destination IP addresses, ports, and protocol information are all included in the state information.

ii. **Connection Tracking**: In addition to tracking the status of active sessions, stateful NAT64 recognizes the context of connections. This makes it possible to handle protocols like FTP where a single session consists of several connections.

iii. **Dynamic Port Allocation**: To manage numerous connections from the same source IPv6 address, stateful NAT64 may dynamically assign ports for translations.

iv. **Use Cases**: Stateful NAT64 is useful for protocols requiring more sophisticated connection tracking and handling, like those involving numerous connections.

v. **Comparison**

Complexity: Stateless NAT64 is less complicated and has less overhead since it does not maintain state.

The complexity of stateful NAT64 increases with the need to monitor and control the state of each translation.

vi. **Scenarios**: Stateless NAT64 functions well in many scenarios, but it may not be compatible with all protocols that require connection tracking.

Stateful NAT64 is advised when more intricate handling is needed, particularly for protocols with numerous or dynamic connections.

In conclusion, the specific requirements of the network and the protocols being used determine either stateful or stateless NAT64 to use. Stateless NAT64 is simpler and more scalable, whereas stateful NAT64 maintains state information for active connections and offers better support for complicated protocols.

Security Considerations in IPv6 Transition

The shift from IPv4 to IPv6 presents several security risks as organizations put different transition strategies in place to make sure the two protocols work together. The following are some of the most important security concerns associated with IPv6 transition techniques that should be taken into consideration.

i. **Tunneling Security**

IPv6 packets are encapsulated within IPv4 packets via tunneling techniques such as 6to4. Attackers may be able to manipulate or intercept packets by taking advantage of flaws in various encapsulation techniques.

Tunnel endpoint security is very important. Traffic can be redirected or altered if an attacker manages to take over a tunnel endpoint.

ii. **Dual Stack Environment**

In a dual-stack setup, running both IPv4 and IPv6 expands the attack surface. Both protocols require security measures to stop weaknesses from being taken advantage of.

Security flaws in the dual-stack environment may arise from misconfigurations. Organizations must make sure that intrusion detection/prevention systems, firewalls, and other security equipment are configured correctly.

iii. **Addressing and Address Resolution**

IPv6 poses new addressing issues, and spoofing attacks can be launched by attackers taking advantage of vulnerabilities in address resolution methods, such as the Neighbor Discovery Protocol (NDP).

Because the IPv6 address space is so large, thorough scanning is more difficult. However, reconnaissance can still be used by attackers to find active hosts.

iv. **Transition Mechanism-Specific Risks**

Relay routers are essential to the 6to4 transition process. These relay routers could be used maliciously by attackers for amplification attacks or traffic interception if they are not secured.

v. **Lack of IPv6 Expertise**

Due to a lack of knowledge about IPv6, many IT professionals may make mistakes in configuration and neglect security measures. Programs for awareness and adequate training are important.

vi. **IPv6 Transition Planning**

There may be security gaps in organizations due to incomplete transition arrangements. Risk assessments, security guidelines, and continuing oversight are all part of a well-organized transition strategy.

Organizations should adopt best practices for IPv6 deployment, prioritize security measures, and carry out in-depth risk assessments to address these issues. Security audits and monitoring regularly are essential to identify and address potential vulnerabilities in the dynamic network architecture.

Deployment Best Practices

When switching from IPv4 to IPv6, implementing IPv6 translation techniques can be crucial to facilitating communication between the two protocols.

The guidelines below can be used to implement IPv6 translation mechanisms in different network environments:

i. **Understand the Transition Requirements**

Your network's transition requirements should be well defined, taking into account things like the number of IPv4 devices, apps, and services that are already in use.

ii. **Choose the Right Translation Mechanism**

Based on the unique requirements of your network, assess and select the best IPv6 translation technique. Dual-Stack, IPv6 over IPv4, and Network Address Translation 64 (NAT64) are examples of common techniques.

iii. **Assess Network Topology and Architecture**

To decide where to put the translation mechanisms in place, examine the architecture and topology of your network. Take into account the IPv4 and IPv6 service locations, as well as the core, distribution, and access layers.

iv. **Implement transition mechanisms**

Use a suitable strategy, such as dual-stack, to enable the coexistence of IPv4 and IPv6. This makes the switchover easier and allows devices to talk to each other using either protocol.

v. **Upgrade Network Devices and Software**

Make sure that IPv6 is compatible with network equipment, such as switches, firewalls, and routers. Download and install the most recent IPv6-compatible firmware or software updates for your devices.

vi. **Configure and Test Translation Mechanisms**

Set up the selected translation mechanism on the appropriate network devices. To confirm that the translation mechanism is operating well and that it satisfies performance requirements, thoroughly test it.

vii. **Consider Security Implications**

Consider the possibility that IPv6 translation procedures have security risks. Put into practice security measures including intrusion detection and prevention systems, stateful firewalls, and suitable access control guidelines.

viii. **Address DNS Considerations**

Make sure that IPv6 is supported by your DNS setup. Set up DNS servers to handle IPv6 addresses' AAAA records. In a dual-stack context, this is essential for correct name resolution.

ix. **Provide Training and Documentation**

Educate support teams, network administrators, and IT staff on the complexities of IPv6 translation techniques. Make extensive documentation to help with upkeep and troubleshooting.

x. **Monitor and Optimize**

To monitor the performance of the IPv6 translation procedures, use network monitoring tools. Regularly review logs and statistics to identify any issues and address them. For greater efficiency and dependability, optimize settings.

xi. **Plan for Future Growth**

Think about how scalable the IPv6 translation method of choice is. Consider how your network will expand in the future and make sure the solution you choose can handle more devices and services.

xii. **Engage with ISPs and Peering Partners**

If necessary, work with peering partners and Internet service providers (ISPs) to offer seamless IPv6 connectivity. Verify whether upstream networks support IPv6 and take care of any necessary setups or modifications.

By following these guidelines, IPv6 translation techniques can be implemented successfully in a range of network scenarios, contributing to a smooth transition from IPv4 to IPv6.

Chapter 5: IPv6 Troubleshooting

IPv6 troubleshooting is becoming increasingly important for network managers and IT professionals as the world transitions to Internet Protocol version 6 (IPv6) to meet the growing number of connected devices. As the successor to IPv4, IPv6 has various benefits, including increased address space and network efficiency. However, the implementation of any new technology necessitates effective troubleshooting to address connectivity issues, configuration errors, and other unforeseen challenges.

Here are several challenges that illustrate the necessity for excellent IPv6 troubleshooting strategies:

5.1 IPv6 Addressing Issues

Address configuration errors

There are several reasons why IPv6 address configuration errors might arise, and they can cause network and communication problems. Here are a few common IPv6 address setting errors, along with suitable illustrations:

i. **Incorrect Address Syntax**

    Error: IPv6 addresses that include incorrect characters or lack colons.

    Illustration: FE80::203:E4FFFE3B:5C4E (incorrect) should be FE80::203:E4FF:FE3B:5C4E

    Comment: The appropriate grouping of hexadecimal digits is disrupted by the absence of colons in the middle.

ii. **Incomplete Address**

    Error: A group or groups of omitted hexadecimal digits

Illustration: 2001:ABCD:CAFE:100:: (incomplete) should be 2001:ABCD:CAFE:100::1

iii. **Multiple Double-Colon Usage**

Error: Using two or more double colons in a single address.

Illustration:2001:ABCD::CAFE:100::1 (multiple double-colons) should be 2001:ABCD: CAFE:100::1

Comment: An IPv6 address cannot contain two double colons (::) since doing so would generate confusion in the address format. To make an IPv6 address simpler to understand, successive blocks of zeros can be compressed using the double colon shorthand notation.

iv. **Invalid Interface ID**

Error: Link-local addresses using an incorrect interface identifier.

Illustration: fe80::95c1%eth2 (incorrect interface identifier) should be fe80::95c1%2

v. **Link-Local Address on the Internet**

Error: Usage of link-local addresses outside the local network.

Illustration: Setting up fe80::1 as the global server address rather than 2001:DB8: DAAD:0001::/64.

vi. **Incorrect Prefix Length**

Error: Incorrectly assigning a subnet's prefix length.

Illustration: 2001: ABCD::CAFE:100: :/48 (incorrect) should be 2001: ABCD: CAFE:100: :/64

Comment: Subnet misalignment, routing failures, and address conflicts are just a few of the problems that might result from an incorrect prefix length.

It's important to keep in mind that improper IPv6 address settings can result in connectivity issues because IPv6 addresses are necessary for networks to operate correctly. Regularly verifying and testing IPv6 configurations helps to provide a robust and secure network environment.

Duplicate Address Detection (DAD)

In IPv6, a method called duplicate address detection (DAD) makes sure that an address assigned to a network interface is distinct within a certain range, like a local link. DAD assists in avoiding conflict resolution, which might result in communication problems. The following are some possible scenarios in which issues with duplicate address detection could arise:

i. **Manual Configuration Errors**

   Scenario: When manually configuring IP addresses on a network, an administrator could accidentally give a device on the same link an IPv6 address that is already in use by another device.

   Problem: The network might experience conflicts and unpredictable behavior without DAD.

ii. **Dynamic Address Assignment**

   Scenario: Many devices can try to set the same address at the same time in scenarios where IPv6 addresses are dynamically assigned (such as Stateless Address Autoconfiguration, or SLAAC).

   Problem: These devices may end up with duplicate addresses without DAD, which would interfere with connectivity.

iii. Network Mobility

Scenario: It is possible for a device moving between links in a mobile network to keep its IPv6 address from one link as it moves to another.

Problem: Conflicts could arise if the device introduced a duplicate address on the new link without DAD.

iv. Unintentional Cloning of Virtual Machines

Scenario: Cloning or duplicating virtual machines (VMs) in virtualized systems increases the possibility that the cloned VMs will try to utilize the same IPv6 address.

Problem: These cloned virtual machines can cause address conflicts and interfere with network connection if DAD isn't used.

v. Temporary Network Connectivity Issues

Scenario: A device is unplugged from the network for a short period and then connected again later.

Problem: Another device can obtain the same IPv6 address during the disconnections. Conflicts may arise when the original device reconnects without DAD.

vi. Network Reconfiguration

Scenario: Unintended address conflicts can arise from changing network configurations through procedures like subnet renumbering or reorganization.

Problem: Devices might not be aware of the changes without DAD, which could result in addressing conflicts.

In each of these cases, Duplicate Address Detection makes sure that devices connected to the same network first confirm that their IPv6 addresses are unique before presuming that they are open for communication. In IPv6 networks, DAD is an essential method for preserving address integrity and averting communication breakdowns.

5.2 Router Configuration and Routing Issues

Router Advertisement (RA) and Router Solicitation (RS)

The IPv6 Neighbor Discovery Protocol's two main components are Router Advertisement (RA) and Router Solicitation (RS). Hosts utilize RS messages to seek configuration information from routers, while routers use RA messages to announce their presence. Network functioning may be impacted by RA and RS issues. Here are a few situations that work well for issues with router solicitation and advertisement:

  i. **Missing Router Advertisements**

  Scenario: Periodically scheduled Router Advertisements are not sent by routers.

  Problem: Routers are not known to hosts, and they are not provided with the necessary configuration data.

  Solution: Make sure that routers are set up correctly to transmit Router Advertisements, troubleshoot router setup, and look for network problems.

  ii. **Unsolicited Router Advertisements**

  Scenario: Too many Router Advertisements are being sent out by routers without permission.

Problem: Host resources and network bandwidth are consumed by excessive RA traffic.

Solution: To prevent unnecessary traffic, modify the router setup parameters to follow the suggested intervals for transmitting router advertisements.

iii. **Router Advertisements with Incorrect Information**

Scenario: Incorrect parameters are sent by routers in Router Advertisements.

Problem: Inaccurate information may be used by hosts to configure themselves, which could cause communication issues.

Solution: Check router configurations and make any necessary corrections. Audit and monitor router marketing parameters regularly.

iv. **Lack of Router Solicitations**

Scenario: To find routers, hosts do not send out router solicitations.

Problem: Routers may not provide hosts with the information they need, which could result in incomplete or inaccurate configuration.

Solution: Examine network connectivity, host setups, and any other problems that might be blocking hosts from submitting router solicitations. Make sure the hosts are set up to conduct solicitation as necessary.

v. **Duplicate Router Advertisements**

Scenario: For the same network, several routers deliver contradicting Router Advertisements.

Problem: Conflicting configuration information may be sent to hosts, which could lead to erratic behavior or problems with connectivity.

Solution: Find and fix router conflict. Ascertain that only authorized routers are transmitting advertisements and that routers are configured appropriately.

vi. **Router Advertisement Spoofing**

Scenario: Fake Router advertisements may be sent by Malicious entities

Problem: There is a danger to security when hosts route traffic through unauthorized routers.

Solution: Use security tools like RA Guard to identify and stop faked router advertisements. To reduce the possibility of man-in-the-middle attacks, implement secure network protocols.

vii. **Network Partitioning**

Scenario: Network partitions hinder the exchange of RA messages between routers on separate segments.

Problem: Routers on the other side of the partition may be invisible to hosts on one side.

Solution: To avoid total network segment isolation, deal with network partition concerns, verify router connectivity, and consider redundancy measures.

viii. **Incomplete Prefix Information**

Scenario: Router Advertisements from routers do not provide the required prefix information.

Problem: Incorrect IPv6 address prefixes could cause hosts to have addressing problems.

Solution: Make sure that the router advertisements contain all required prefix information by reviewing the router parameters to verify that prefixes are correctly defined and distributed.

Router Advertisement and Solicitation issues can be efficiently prevented and addressed with the support of proactive configuration reviews, routine monitoring, and adherence to best practices for IPv6 network management.

Dynamic routing protocols Issues.

To allow routers to interchange routing information dynamically and adjust to changes in network topology, dynamic routing protocols are crucial to networking. But problems do happen, and these are some situations and possible fixes for them:

i. **Route Convergence Delays**

    Scenario: When there are topology changes, the network takes longer to update its routing tables.

    Solution

    Optimize timers: To reduce convergence delays, modify the hello and dead intervals in the routing protocol.

    Route summarization: To accelerate convergence, summarize routes at network borders to minimize the number of routes exchanged.

ii. **Routing Loops**

    Scenario: Routing loops can result in poor routing or even network failures.

Solution

Split Horizon: Use split horizon to stop routers from promoting routes that lead back to the interfaces they originally learned.

Route Poisoning: To prevent loops, use route poisoning or route hold-down techniques to notify routers about unavailable routes.

iii. **Link Flapping:**

Scenario: Routing tables are constantly updated by routers due to frequent changes in link state.

Solution

Interface stabilization: To stabilize communications and cut down on pointless route updates, modify interface characteristics like timers and bandwidth.

Route dampening: To avoid unnecessary updates, use route dampening to reduce updates for routes that change frequently.

iv. **Suboptimal Routing**

Scenario: The routing protocol calculates metrics inefficiently, it therefore selects pathways that are not optimal.

Solution

Metric adjustments: Adjust the weights of the metrics to better represent the real network conditions and give priority to the desired paths.

Put into practice policy-based routing: To impact route selection based on particular parameters, like source or destination IP addresses, use policies.

v. **Routing Information Overload**

Scenario: Networks on a large scale may experience problems with too much routing information.

Solution

Route summarization: To minimize the amount of entries in routing tables, summarize routes at network borders.

Put route filtering into practice: Reduce the number of routes that are shared by filtering out the ones that aren't necessary.

vi. **Security Concerns:**

Scenario: Unauthorized routers make an effort to take part in routing.

Solution

Authentication: To confirm the validity of routing changes, enable authentication features in the routing protocol.

Employ filtering for routing protocols: To stop illegal routers from taking part, filter routing updates based on source IP addresses or other parameters.

vii. **Resource Utilization**

Scenario: Dynamic routing protocols use a lot of memory and CPU power.

Solution

Hardware upgrades: Upgrade router hardware to handle the increased load.

Protocol-specific optimizations: Implement protocol-specific optimizations and features provided by the router vendor

It's critical to employ diagnostic tools, examine network traffic, and analyze logs to pinpoint and fix specific issues when troubleshooting dynamic routing protocol problems.

5.3 Firewall and Security Concerns

In an IPv6 system, incorrectly configured firewalls might result in security flaws and connectivity problems. In an IPv6 network, the following are common scenarios and possible fixes for incorrect firewall configurations:

i. **Scenario: All IPv6 traffic is blocked by default deny policy.**

   Issue: The firewall is set up with an IPv6 deny policy by default, which blocks all traffic, including communication that is authorized.

   Solution: Modify the firewall policy to allow IPv6 traffic that is required. Determine which ports and services are necessary, then establish clear rules to permit them. Make sure that the firewall rules adhere to the least privilege principle and are clearly described.

ii. **Scenario: Incorrectly Configured Stateful Inspection for IPv6**

   Issue: It is possible for stateful inspection, which keeps track of connections, to be incorrectly configured, which could cause problems for both new and existing connections.

   Solution: Examine and modify the stateful inspection configurations. Verify that the firewall is tracking IPv6 connections accurately. Examine any special guidelines that apply to managing stateful connections and make any necessary adjustments.

iii. **Scenario: Missing or Incorrect IPv6 Rules**

Issue: IPv6 firewall rules are either missing or misconfigured, which stops some kinds of traffic from going through.

Solution: Examine and update the IPv6 firewall rules with great care. Verify the presence and accuracy of rules that permit necessary services, such as DNS (UDP/53), HTTP (TCP/80), and HTTPS (TCP/443). If necessary, take into account application-specific rules.

iv. **Scenario: Improper Handling of ICMPv6**

Issue: The firewall may be blocking ICMPv6 traffic randomly, interfering with IPv6 path MTU finding and other critical tasks.

Solution: Allow the appropriate ICMPv6 traffic over the firewall. ICMPv6 is critical to the proper operation of IPv6, including the Path MTU Discovery mechanism. Adjust the firewall rules to allow ICMPv6 types that are required for network operations.

v. **Scenario: Inadequate Logging Configuration**

Issue: The firewall may not be configured to properly log IPv6 traffic, making it difficult to detect problems and monitor security incidents.

Solution: Configure the firewall to log any relevant IPv6 traffic. Logging can be extremely useful for detecting and analyzing security problems. Adjust log levels and analyze logs regularly to look for any unexpected or suspicious activities.

vi. **Scenario: Lack of IPv6 Address Filtering**

Issue: The firewall may not be set up to filter traffic based on IPv6 addresses, resulting in potential security concerns.

Solution: Set up address-based filtering rules in the firewall to manage traffic based on source and destination IPv6 addresses. This improves security by limiting access to specified hosts or networks.

vii. **Scenario: Zone-based Firewall Misconfiguration**

Issue: When implementing zone-based firewalls, incorrect zone definition and assignment can result in unwanted traffic limits or allowances.

Solution: Check the firewall configuration's zone definitions and assignments. Ensure that interfaces are correctly assigned to the right zones and that zone-based policies meet the required security requirements.

viii. **Scenario: IPv6 Tunneling Issues**

Issue: Firewalls may not be properly set to handle IPv6 tunneling technologies (such as 6to4 and Teredo).

Solution: If the network design includes IPv6 tunneling methods, modify the firewall rules to allow them. Consider whether tunneling is required for your network, or if native IPv6 access is available.

Firewall settings should be audited and tested regularly to ensure that they comply with security rules and best practices. Documentation and change control procedures are critical for maintaining a safe and well-configured firewall in an IPv6 environment.

Security Policies affecting IPv6 traffic

IPv6 traffic security is an important part of network administration. Security policies serve to secure the confidentiality, integrity, and availability of information. Here are some problems and answers regarding security regulations affecting IPv6 traffic:

i. **Scenario: Lack of IPv6-specific Security Policies**

    Issue: IPv6 traffic may not be specifically addressed by security policies, which could result in oversight and possible vulnerabilities.

    Solution: Create and put into effect thorough security guidelines that handle IPv6 traffic in particular. Firewall rules, intrusion detection and prevention, encryption, and other IPv6-specific security measures should all be covered by these regulations.

ii. **Scenario: Inconsistent Security Policies Between IPv4 and IPv6**

    Issue: Inconsistencies and possible security holes may result from different IPv4 and IPv6 security settings.

    Solution: Make sure that IPv4 and IPv6 environments use the same security policies. To maintain a consistent security posture, apply the same policies, procedures, and safeguards to both IP versions.

iii. **Scenario: Insufficient Authentication and Authorization for IPv6 Services**

    Issue: For IPv6 services, inadequate or nonexistent authorization and authentication procedures might result in misuse or illegal access.

    Solution: Put robust permission and authentication mechanisms in place for IPv6 services. For central user authentication, make use of protocols such as LDAP or RADIUS. To limit access to services

101

based on user roles and responsibilities, apply access control lists (ACLs).

iv. **Scenario: Unencrypted IPv6 Traffic**

Issue: Sensitive data may be transferred in plaintext during IPv6 transmission, making it vulnerable to possible eavesdropping.

Solution: Enforce IPv6 traffic to be encrypted, particularly for important services like file transfers, email, and online applications. To ensure secure communication between network devices, use protocols such as IPsec.

v. **Scenario: Inadequate IPv6 Address Filtering**

Issue: Inadequate IPv6 address-based filtering may result in denial-of-service attacks or illegal access.

Solution: Firewalls and routers can regulate traffic based on source and destination IPv6 addresses by implementing address-based filtering. Utilize ACLs to control traffic flow according to security standards and address range restrictions.

vi. **Scenario: Misconfigured IPv6 Access Controls**

Issue: When access control lists (ACLs) and other access restrictions are implemented incorrectly, they might permit unauthorized traffic and obstruct lawful communication.

Solution: Audit and examine IPv6 ACL setups regularly. Make sure that security regulations and business requirements are appropriately reflected in ACLs. ACLs should be tested to ensure their efficacy without interfering with vital services.

vii. **Scenario: Lack of IPv6 Intrusion Detection and Prevention**

Issue: Because there are no specialized mechanisms for detecting and preventing IPv6 intrusions, attempts to compromise IPv6 communications may go unnoticed.

Solution: Install intrusion detection and prevention systems designed specifically for IPv6 to keep an eye out for and defend against any threats. Make sure that the most recent threat intelligence is consistently added to these platforms.

viii. **Scenario: Insufficient Logging and Monitoring for IPv6**

Issue: Determining security issues could be more challenging if there is insufficient IPv6 traffic logging and monitoring.

Solution: Enhance the features for recording and monitoring IPv6 traffic. Keep track of relevant security events, do regular log analysis, and configure alerting systems to respond promptly to any suspicious activity.

ix. **Scenario: Limited IPv6 Security Training and Awareness**

Issue: Employees might not be trained or aware of IPv6-specific security concerns and acceptable practices.

Solution: Provide IT employees and end users thorough training on IPv6 security. Make sure that staff members are informed of the special difficulties related to IPv6 security and that security policies are conveyed clearly.

x. **Scenario: Lack of Regular Security Audits and Assessments**

Issue: Security policies that are out of date or ineffective may be the result of infrequent security audits and assessments.

Solution: Perform routine IPv6 traffic-specific security audits and evaluations. Determine and fix vulnerabilities, update policies as necessary, and make sure that security measures continue to be effective in the face of changing threats.

To keep an IPv6 environment strong and secure, security policies must be updated and improved regularly. Training and awareness campaigns must also be continued.

5.4 Transition Mechanism Problems
Transitioning from IPv4 to IPv6 challenges

Transitioning from IPv4 to IPv6 presents various issues, including the necessity to support both protocols during the migration process. Here are some common cases and appropriate solutions for the issues related to the transition from IPv4 to IPv6:

i. **Scenario: Address Exhaustion in IPv4**

Issue: IPv4 address exhaustion is a serious problem, particularly when IP addresses become more and more in demand.

Solution: Transition to IPv6 to avoid address exhaustion. Create a complete migration strategy that covers addressing, routing, and DNS considerations. Consider using dual-stack or tunneling technologies to assist in a gradual transition.

ii. **Scenario: Dual-Stack Operational Challenges**

Issue: Running IPv4 and IPv6 concurrently (dual stack) might complicate operations and increase administrative overhead.

Solution: Start with essential network components or services and gradually implement dual-stack. Ascertain that the applications, devices, and network infrastructure are all IPv6 capable. Train IT staff on managing dual-stack environments and use automation tools to streamline the transition.

iii. **Scenario: DNS Transition Challenges**

Issue: It can be difficult to transition DNS infrastructure to support IPv6, particularly when zone file management and DNSSEC are involved.

Solution: DNS servers should be updated to IPv6-compatible versions and set up to handle both IPv4 and IPv6 requests. To update DNS entries, add AAAA records for hosts that support IPv6. To make sure everything is working properly, test DNS resolution for both IPv4 and IPv6.

The transition from IPv4 to IPv6 is a difficult process that necessitates careful planning, continuous testing, and collaboration among numerous stakeholders. By addressing these issues with proper solutions, enterprises can successfully manage the hurdles and reap the benefits of IPv6.

Issues with dual-stack configurations

In dual-stack configurations, network infrastructure runs IPv4 and IPv6 concurrently. Dual-stack makes the switch from IPv4 to IPv6 seamless, however, there are a few drawbacks. The following situations and fixes for problems with dual-stack setups are provided:

i. **Scenario: Inconsistent Routing for IPv4 and IPv6**

    Issue: Inconsistent IPv4 and IPv6 routing configurations might result in traffic diversion or less-than-ideal routing.

    Solution: Make sure that IPv4 and IPv6 routing tables are set up correctly. Verify routing protocols such as EIGRP or OSPF are set up correctly to advertise and choose routes for both IP versions.

ii. **Scenario: Address Misallocation or Conflicts**

    Issue: Network instability or connection issues may result from misallocation or inconsistent addressing.

    Solution: Allocating IPv4 and IPv6 addresses needs to be carefully planned and reviewed. Avoid conflicts and overlaps between IPv4 and IPv6 address ranges. Periodically review and update the address plans in response to network changes.

iii. **Scenario: Firewalls Blocking One IP Version**

    Issue: Firewalls that aren't configured correctly can let through traffic from one IP version but not from another.

    Solution: Examine firewall configurations to ensure that IPv4 and IPv6 rules are applied consistently. Make sure both IP versions are sufficiently covered by the policies, stateful inspection rules, and access control lists (ACLs).

iv. **Scenario: IPv6-only Devices on a Dual-Stack Network**

Issue: If there are problems with IPv4 coexistence, IPv6-only devices could find it difficult to communicate over a dual-stack network.

Solution: Make sure that IPv6-only devices can be handled by dual-stack network components with ease. Make sure switches, routers, and other infrastructure elements can route traffic for both IP versions in the right way.

v. **Scenario: Quality of Service (QoS) Configurations**

Issue: Improperly configured QoS settings may affect traffic prioritizing for both IPv4 and IPv6.

Solution: To accommodate both IPv4 and IPv6 traffic, review and modify QoS policies. To guarantee an equitable and effective utilization of network resources, prioritize crucial services and applications uniformly for both IP versions.

vi. **Scenario: Suboptimal Load Balancing for Dual-Stack Servers**

Issue: Resource utilization may be uneven as a result of load balancing settings that do not distribute traffic between IPv4 and IPv6 servers equally.

Solution: For both IP versions, distribute traffic efficiently by optimizing load balancing setups. Ascertain that load balancers are aware of the IPv4 and IPv6 servers' capacity.

vii. **Scenario: Lack of Monitoring and Troubleshooting Tools**

Issue: IPv6 problems may take longer to resolve if monitoring and troubleshooting tools are inadequate.

Solution: Configure and verify IPv6-capable monitoring tools regularly. Equip network administrators with resources to detect and fix dual-stack problems as well as training on IPv6-specific troubleshooting methods.

viii. **Scenario: Security Policy Gaps in Dual-Stack Networks**

Issue: There may be vulnerabilities if security policies do not sufficiently cover IPv4 and IPv6.

Solution: Review and update security policies regularly to include both IP versions. Make sure that IPv4 and IPv6 traffic are equally protected by security mechanisms such as firewalls, intrusion detection/prevention systems, and access controls.

To ensure a reliable and secure dual-stack network, meticulous planning, continuous monitoring, and frequent testing are necessary. When these situations are resolved, IPv4 and IPv6 in a dual-stack environment will function more dependable and effectively.

5.5 Best Practices for IPv6 Troubleshooting

Preventing common problems in IPv6 troubleshooting entails taking proactive steps to ensure the smooth and effective operation of IPv6 networks. Here are some preventive measures you can take:

Thorough Planning and Design

Do a thorough network assessment and meticulously plan the IPv6 deployment before putting it into use. Think about subnetting, address space distribution, and the IPv6 addressing scheme.

Education and Training

Educate engineers, support personnel, and network administrators about IPv6 principles, addressing, and troubleshooting methods.

Make sure everyone in the IT department understands IPv6 security best practices.

Dual-Stack Implementation

Implement dual-stack architecture to accommodate IPv4 and IPv6 concurrently.

This lessens interruptions throughout the migration process and permits a smooth transition.

Regular Audits and Assessments:

Make sure that IPv6 configurations are in line with the network architecture by conducting audits regularly.

Review security policies regularly and make any necessary updates.

Monitoring and Logging

Put in place reliable monitoring systems that can follow IPv6 traffic, look for anomalies, and send out notifications when something might go wrong.

Set up logging to capture events connected to IPv6 for subsequent examination.

Firewall Configuration

To support IPv6 traffic, update the firewall rules.

Make sure that IPv6 firewall settings are just as stringent and safe as IPv4 firewall settings.

Router Advertisement (RA) Guard

Implement RA protection mechanisms on network devices to avoid rogue router ads.

This helps to prevent man-in-the-middle attacks, which can occur through unauthorized routers.

Intrusion Detection and Prevention Systems (IDPS)

Implement IDPS systems with IPv6 traffic monitoring and protection capabilities.

Update rule sets and signatures to identify and stop new threats.

Quality of Service (QoS) Implementation

To prioritize IPv6 traffic according to application requirements, configure QoS settings.

Make sure that crucial IPv6 applications run smoothly and dependably.

Regular Firmware and Software Updates

Update networking hardware, such as switches and routers, with the most recent software and firmware versions. To fix vulnerabilities, quickly apply security patches.

IPv6 Security Best Practices

Follow IPv6 security best practices, which include employing encryption, segmenting your network, and imposing robust authentication procedures. You can build a strong IPv6 infrastructure that is less vulnerable to typical problems by implementing these preventative steps, and you'll be better prepared to troubleshoot and handle any problems that may come up. Your

IPv6 network's continued security and stability can be ensured by routinely assessing and updating these procedures.

About the Author

Am an expert in knowledge empowerment with substantial training and teaching experience in information, communication, and technology. I possess an array of experiences that I apply to my professional career. These include positions such as Oracle Academy Instructor, Cisco Systems Academic Instructor, Certified Lead Trainer, and ICDL Trainer of Trainers. My unwavering devotion to sharing information propels me beyond the boundaries of traditional education. With my unmatched teaching abilities, I expertly guide students through the complexity of technology, delivering precision and clarity. Many people follow in my footsteps, earning the knowledge and confidence required to pass certification exams and excel in their respective areas. My influence extends well beyond the classroom. As an examiner and IT practitioner for managed services, I carefully assess the changing environment of skills, ensuring that my guidance remains at the forefront of industry standards. With a diverse background that encompasses end-user computing, system administration, programming, and database management, I shape the goals of young professionals, molding them into competent experts in their respective fields. My passion for sharing information goes beyond the boundaries of conventional teaching methods. I exemplify the pinnacle of IT expertise, seamlessly blending conceptual understanding with practical implementation. I strive to provide my customers with a true sense of joy and purpose as they work toward realizing their goals.

Acknowledgment

In honor of my dear family

For the countless hours spent on this book's research, writing, and editing as well as for your continued support, inspiration, and understanding. I've always been inspired by your love and patience.

In honor of my dear clientele

I appreciate your trust in entrusting me with your networking requirements and difficulties. These pages' insights have been influenced by your queries, comments, and practical experiences. To serve you is a privilege.

All of you have my sincere gratitude and appreciation as I dedicate this book to you

www.ingramcontent.com/pod-product-compliance
Lightning Source LLC
Chambersburg PA
CBHW071255050326
40690CB00011B/2409